Implementing Cloud Storage with OpenStack Swift

Design, implement, and successfully manage your own cloud storage cluster using the popular OpenStack Swift software

Amar Kapadia

Sreedhar Varma

Kris Rajana

open source*
community experience distilled

[PACKT]
PUBLISHING

BIRMINGHAM - MUMBAI

Implementing Cloud Storage with OpenStack Swift

First published: May 2014

Production Reference: 1090514

Published by Packt Publishing Ltd.
Livery Place
35 Livery Street
Birmingham B3 2PB, UK.

ISBN 978-1-78216-805-8

www.packtpub.com

Cover Image by Seenivasan Kumaravel (kseenivasan@hotmail.com)

Credits

Authors
  Amar Kapadia

  Sreedhar Varma

  Kris Rajana

Reviewers
  Juan J. Martínez

  Sriram Subramanian

  Alex Yang

Commissioning Editor
  Kartikey Pandey

Acquisition Editor
  Harsha Bharwani

Content Development Editor
  Priyanka S

Technical Editor
  Faisal Siddiqui

Copy Editors
  Janbal Dharmaraj

  Sayanee Mukherjee

  Aditya Nair

  Alfida Paiva

Project Coordinator
  Puja Shukla

Proofreaders
  Maria Gould

  Ameesha Green

  Paul Hindle

Indexer
  Mariammal Chettiyar

Graphics
  Ronak Dhruv

  Abhinash Sahu

Production Coordinator
  Alwin Roy

Cover Work
  Alwin Roy

Foreword

I have worked with Amar in the OpenStack San Francisco Bay Area user group and the Entertainment Technology Council cloud effort over the past year. Amar is part of the larger Seagate and Evault effort to transform a manufacturer and product commodity vendor. He has been working with Swift for around 3 years and has deep understanding of what makes it tick.

The authors, like myself, have been lured into the great experiment that is OpenStack and it has changed our careers for the better. Seagate, EVault, and Vedams are working to provide higher-level services like key value store disks and API implementations that provide novel solutions for software defined infrastructure problems. The authors have produced an excellent operational guide that will benefit anyone interested in understanding Swift.

Object storage predates the implementations of Swift and S3. It originated in the universities and spread to Internet based companies such as Yahoo and Google. Internet companies require vast amounts of eventually consistent data. As the business of search changed the way the technology industry thought about services, more uses for object stores were found. Swift was publicly released about a year after Rackspace started working on the CloudFiles replacement in August 2009. The development was born out of a tight group that blended development and operations expertise. Rackspace needed massively scalable storage that they had control over the implementation and the code base.

We are very fortunate that at the time Swift was being released to the world as a new open source project in the summer of 2010, NASA engineers were finishing up their rewrite of the virtual server software Eucalyptus. Nova, as the NASA project became known, had an engineering effort that was so similar to Swift, that both teams were stunned. NASA engineer, Joshua McKenty, noted, "We were using the same tools. We had made the same language decisions. We got the two development teams together — none of whom had ever met each other — and we both said: 'Wow, you just wrote the code that we were going to write.'" - http://www.wired.com/2012/04/openstack-histor/.

It was more than just luck that the two teams were developing similar code in a similar fashion. Similar minds came to similar conclusions. I first met Joshua McKenty, Jesse Andrews, and Vishvananda Ishaya, in May 2010. We were all at the MSST storage conference in Incline Village, NV. They were debating over the few nights available to us of what storage to use for their project. I provided some backdrop for Yahoo's storage options. Many drinks later and a few days, it seemed that they were no closer to deciding between the choices available at the time. Just a month later, Rackspace and NASA were to begin down the road of making history.

Swift is an open source private object store for companies seeking to be part of the open source software defined infrastructure movement. Storage APIs breed innovative new ways to develop and operate. Lifting the restrictions of POSIX interfaces has been cathartic. This remote storage model breaks down, however, when you factor in latency and the network cost of repatriating your data. As John Dickenson states, "Storage is key. It always grows. It is incredibly sticky. It is very hard to move around." - `https://www.youtube.com/watch?v=Dd7wmJCDh4w`.

Swift fills this gap of local, simple object storage. It is open source, eventually consistent, supports ACLs, large objects, failure domains, and both Swift and S3 APIs. Using simple, inexpensive servers it drives the cost down below many other vendor backed solutions. While listing off features and direct benefits is a fun exercise, the hidden benefits of using Swift are the most important. Once you start down the path of using Swift and other OpenStack projects, you are on your way to automating your infrastructure.

To properly operate distributed computing software like Swift; you will need to embrace automating your infrastructure using DevOps techniques. DevOps simply means your operations engineers must have development abilities. This is not a new idea, but making it a requirement for operations is. Additionally, when using open source software, your engineers must understand and participate in the open source community that builds and maintains Swift. I have personally built storage systems. The planning, implementation, and operations are always more complicated than expected. This is generally due to the fact of integration. Even if Swift is the first storage solution your company is implementing, you will need to expand, upgrade, and support many generations of Swift. This one facet of your evolving engineering team means your most valuable resources are your engineers, not your vendor relationships. Now even more than in the past, we are moving away from the logic and intelligence buried in the vendor's hardware.

The accomplishment of unshackling customers from the whims of vendors is grand, but it requires a renewed understanding of the value of key personnel and your partnership with the open source community. The CAPEX that would be plowed into the next generation of vendor X hardware now needs to be redirected into keeping your engineers close and committed. The commitment to DevOps engineering means focusing on OPEX to reap the innovation and cost savings from using open source software. In-house software development practices will need be adopted and curated. Consistent code releases to follow the pace of the open source community will work to encourage lasting positive DevOps behaviors. Your infrastructure workplace will be practicing some form of agile development methods. Continuous Integration pipelines and Kanban boards will be your weapons to tame the new business model.

This book gives you a powerful taste of what your DevOps software defined infrastructure will need to thrive and survive. Swift will be your inexpensive, easily expanded distributed storage system that is the backbone of your operations.

Sean Roberts
Board Director at the OpenStack Foundation,
Infrastructure Strategy at Yahoo

About the Authors

Amar Kapadia is a storage technologist and blogger based in the San Francisco Bay Area. He is currently the Senior Director of Strategy for EVault's Long-Term Storage Service, a subsidiary of Seagate. With over 20 years of experience in storage, server, and I/O technologies at Emulex, Philips, and HP, Amar's current passion is cloud and object storage technologies based on OpenStack Swift. He holds a Master's degree in Electrical Engineering from the University of California, Berkeley.

When not working on OpenStack Swift, Amar can be found working on Open Compute Platform technologies, MongoDB, PHP, AJAX, or jQuery. Amar's blogs can be found at buildcloudstorage.com.

I would like to thank my wife for tolerating my late night and weekend book-writing sessions. I would also like to thank the Long-Term Storage Service team at EVault who generously helped provide content and critique on various chapters.

Sreedhar Varma has more than 15 years of experience in the storage industry, developing storage software and solutions. He has worked on various storage technologies (such as SCSI, SAS, SATA, and FC), HBA drivers (Adaptec, Emulex, Qlogic, Promise, and so on), RAID, and storage stacks of various operating systems. He was involved in building system software for Stratus Fault Tolerant and High Availability systems. He has good working experience with SAN, NAS, and iSCSI networks as well as various storage arrays (Dothill, IBM, EMC, Hitachi, and Oracle Pillar). Sreedhar is currently involved with object storage implementations (Swift, Ceph) and developing software using corresponding REST APIs.

Sreedhar has a Master's degree in Computer Science from the University of Massachusetts.

He is presently working for Vedams Software (providing storage engineering services). In the past, he has worked for Stratus Technologies, Compaq, Digital Equipment Corp, and IBM.

I would like to thank my wife for her support and encouragement while I was writing the chapters for this book. I would also like to acknowledge the assistance of Vedams and EVault OpenStack teams in building and managing an OpenStack cluster. This enabled us to verify every aspect coved in this book, including installation, testing, and tuning with clear instructions on how-to.

Kris Rajana is an entrepreneur, passionate in building globally distributed teams to develop and maintain innovative products and solutions. His areas of interests include tape, DAS, NAS, SAN, and fast emerging technologies (Cloud, SDN, SDS, and Flash Arrays). Kris has over 20 years of experience in managing engineering teams in areas including space and aviation at BFGoodrich Aerospace and storage at Snap Appliance (currently Overland Storage) Adaptec, Xyratex, and Sullego. Currently, as the CEO of Vedams, Kris takes immense pride in his team and its development that leads to execution excellence. Kris's current passion is application of Big Data concepts to improve reliability and uptime of systems.

Kris is a student and sevak at San Jose Chinmaya Mission. Kris also serves on the board of the Pratham Bay Area Chapter. Kris and Vedams sponsor the Pratham Urban Learning Center in Hyderabad.

Kris earned his doctorate in engineering science from the Pennsylvania State University and keeps abreast with emerging management methodologies through his affiliation with Stanford University.

I would like to thank my family for their encouragement. Finally, I would like to thank the Vedams team and my mentors over the years.

About the Reviewers

Juan J. Martínez is an experienced software developer with a strong open source background, and has been involved in OpenStack Object Storage since the Bexar release. His work, related to Swift, includes the customization and deployment of Memstore, winner of the UK Cloud Awards 2014 organized by Cloud Pro magazine, and a number of open source projects to provide access to the storage using common file transfer protocols (FTP and SFTP). He's currently employed by Memset, a British cloud provider based in Cranleigh.

Sriram Subramanian is the founder and cloud specialist at Cloud Don LLC, a cloud consulting firm that offers cloud services. He is an OpenStack enthusiast, passionate about OpenStack's success. Previously, he was a lead developer at ComputeNext building a Federated Cloud Marketplace. Here, he gained expertise in multiple cloud platforms including OpenStack. Prior to ComputeNext, he was with various companies such as Microsoft, Intel, and Hitachi, working on a wide spectrum of technologies such as cloud computing, virtualization, compilers, and low power design. He is passionate about cloud computing, green/clean technology, and holistic living.

Alex Yang is a software engineer in cloud computing. In his previous company, Sina App Engine, the biggest PaaS service provider in China, Alex developed the storage service based on OpenStack Swift. There are 500,000 developers in Sina App Engine, who use the storage service to host web images or archive logs.

Alex also has experience working on network virtualization, software defined network, and distributed storage.

www.PacktPub.com

Support files, eBooks, discount offers and more

You might want to visit www.PacktPub.com for support files and downloads related to your book.

Did you know that Packt offers eBook versions of every book published, with PDF and ePub files available? You can upgrade to the eBook version at www.PacktPub.com and as a print book customer, you are entitled to a discount on the eBook copy. Get in touch with us at service@packtpub.com for more details.

At www.PacktPub.com, you can also read a collection of free technical articles, sign up for a range of free newsletters and receive exclusive discounts and offers on Packt books and eBooks.

http://PacktLib.PacktPub.com

Do you need instant solutions to your IT questions? PacktLib is Packt's online digital book library. Here, you can access, read and search across Packt's entire library of books.

Why Subscribe?

- Fully searchable across every book published by Packt
- Copy and paste, print and bookmark content
- On demand and accessible via web browser

Free Access for Packt account holders

If you have an account with Packt at www.PacktPub.com, you can use this to access PacktLib today and view nine entirely free books. Simply use your login credentials for immediate access.

Table of Contents

Preface

CIOs around the world are asking their teams to take advantage of cloud technologies as a way to slash costs and improve usability. OpenStack is a fast-growing open source cloud software with a number of projects. Swift is one such project that allows users to build cloud storage. With Swift, not only can users build storage using inexpensive commodity hardware, but they can also use the public cloud storage built using the same technology. Starting with the fundamentals of cloud storage and OpenStack Swift, this book will provide you with the skills to build and operate your own cloud storage or use a third-party cloud. This book is an invaluable tool if you want to get a head start in the world of cloud storage using OpenStack Swift. The readers of this book will be equipped to build an on-premise private cloud, manage it, and tune it.

What this book covers

Chapter 1, Cloud Storage – Why Can't I be Like Google?, introduces the need for cloud storage, the underlying technology of object storage, and an extremely popular open source object storage project called OpenStack Swift.

Chapter 2, OpenStack Swift Architecture, discusses the internals of the Swift architecture in detail and shows how elegantly Swift converts commodity hardware into reliable and scalable cloud storage.

Chapter 3, Installing OpenStack Swift, walks you through all the necessary steps required to perform a multi-node Swift installation and how to set it up along with the Keystone setup for authentication.

Chapter 4, Using Swift, describes the various ways you can access Swift object storage. It also provides examples for the various access methods.

Chapter 5, Managing Swift, provides details on the various options that are available to monitor and manage a Swift cluster. Some of the topics covered in this chapter include StatsD metrics, handling drive failures, node failures, and migrations.

Chapter 6, Choosing the Right Hardware, provides you with the information necessary to make the right decision in selecting the required hardware for your cloud setup.

Chapter 7, Tuning Your Swift Installation, walks you through a performance benchmarking tool and the basic mechanisms available to tune a Swift cluster. Users utilizing Swift will need to tune their installation to optimize performance, durability, and availability, based on their unique workload.

Chapter 8, Additional Resources, explores several use cases of Swift and provides pointers on operating systems, virtualization, and distribution tools being used across various Swift installations.

Appendix, Advanced Features, provides details on various commands that can be run from a Swift CLI session.

What you need for this book

The various software components required to follow the instructions in the chapters are as follows:

- Ubuntu Operating System 12.04
    - `http://www.ubuntu.com/download/server`
    - `http://releases.ubuntu.com/12.04/`
- OpenStack Swift Havana release
- python-swiftclient Swift CLI
- cURL
- Swift tools such as Swift-Recon, Swift-Informant, and Swift-Dispersion
- A StatsD server
    - `https://github.com/etsy/statsd/`

Who this book is for

This book is targeted at IT and storage administrators who want to enter the world of cloud storage using OpenStack Swift. It also targets anyone who wishes to understand how to use OpenStack Swift and developers looking to port their applications to OpenStack Swift.

This book also provides invaluable information for IT management professionals trying to understand the differences between traditional and cloud storage.

Conventions

In this book, you will find a number of styles of text that distinguish between different kinds of information. Here are some examples of these styles and an explanation of their meaning.

Code words in text, database table names, folder names, filenames, file extensions, pathnames, dummy URLs, user input, and Twitter handles are shown as follows:

"Typically, a user sends their HTTP GET, PUT, POST, or DELETE request to a set of nodes, and the request is translated to physical nodes by the object storage software."

A block of code is set as follows:

```
import org.jclouds.openstack.swift.CommonSwiftAsyncClient;
import org.jclouds.openstack.swift.CommonSwiftClient;

BlobStoreContext context = ContextBuilder.newBuilder(provider)
            .endpoint("http://LTS2Server/")
            .credentials(user, password)
            .modules(modules)
            .buildView(BlobStoreContext.class);
```

When we wish to draw your attention to a particular part of a code block, the relevant lines or items are set in bold:

```
import org.jclouds.openstack.swift.CommonSwiftAsyncClient;
import org.jclouds.openstack.swift.CommonSwiftClient;

BlobStoreContext context = ContextBuilder.newBuilder(provider)
            .endpoint("http://LTS2Server/")
            .credentials(user, password)
            .modules(modules)
            .buildView(BlobStoreContext.class);
```

Any command-line input or output is written as follows:

```
# curl -X GET -i https://storage.lts2.evault.com/v1/xyz -H 'X-Auth_token:
token'
```

New terms and **important words** are shown in bold.

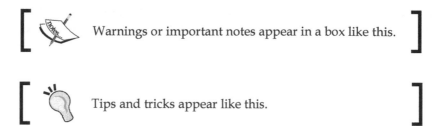

> Warnings or important notes appear in a box like this.

> Tips and tricks appear like this.

Reader feedback

Feedback from our readers is always welcome. Let us know what you think about this book—what you liked or may have disliked. Reader feedback is important for us to develop titles that you really get the most out of.

To send us general feedback, simply send an e-mail to feedback@packtpub.com, and mention the book title via the subject of your message.

If there is a topic that you have expertise in and you are interested in either writing or contributing to a book, see our author guide on www.packtpub.com/authors.

Customer support

Now that you are the proud owner of a Packt book, we have a number of things to help you to get the most from your purchase.

Downloading the example code

You can download the example code files for all Packt books you have purchased from your account at http://www.packtpub.com. If you purchased this book elsewhere, you can visit http://www.packtpub.com/support and register to have the files e-mailed directly to you.

Errata

Although we have taken every care to ensure the accuracy of our content, mistakes do happen. If you find a mistake in one of our books — maybe a mistake in the text or the code — we would be grateful if you would report this to us. By doing so, you can save other readers from frustration and help us improve subsequent versions of this book. If you find any errata, please report them by visiting http://www.packtpub.com/submit-errata, selecting your book, clicking on the **errata submission form** link, and entering the details of your errata. Once your errata are verified, your submission will be accepted and the errata will be uploaded on our website, or added to any list of existing errata, under the Errata section of that title. Any existing errata can be viewed by selecting your title from http://www.packtpub.com/support.

Piracy

Piracy of copyright material on the Internet is an ongoing problem across all media. At Packt, we take the protection of our copyright and licenses very seriously. If you come across any illegal copies of our works, in any form, on the Internet, please provide us with the location address or website name immediately so that we can pursue a remedy.

Please contact us at copyright@packtpub.com with a link to the suspected pirated material.

We appreciate your help in protecting our authors, and our ability to bring you valuable content.

Questions

You can contact us at questions@packtpub.com if you are having a problem with any aspect of the book, and we will do our best to address it.

1

Cloud Storage: Why Can't I be like Google?

If you could build your IT systems and operations from scratch today, would you recreate what you have? That's the question Geir Ramleth, CIO of construction giant Bechtel, asked himself in 2005. The answer was obviously not, and Bechtel ended up using best practices from four Internet forerunners of the time, YouTube, Google, Amazon.com, and Salesforce.com, to create their next set of datacenters. This is exactly the same question CIOs around the world are asking themselves, and that's what cloud storage is about! Through this book, you will learn how to implement a storage system that uses the best practices of these web giants rather than a traditional enterprise, thus cutting **Total Cost of Ownership (TCO)** by more than 10 times. This type of storage is called **cloud storage**.

The following are some key elements that constitute cloud storage:

- Benefits:
    - Dramatic reduction in TCO
    - Unlimited scalability
    - Elasticity achieved by virtualization
    - On-demand; that is, pay for what you use
    - Universal access from anywhere

- Limitations:
    - Sharing storage with other departments or companies
    - Is not a high-performance option
    - Requires a cloud gateway or an application change

Elements of cloud storage

Let us review the benefits and limitations of cloud storage in more detail.

Reduced TCO

Reduced TCO is the crux of cloud storage. Unless this new storage cuts storage cost by more than 10 times, it is not worth switching from block or file storage and dealing with something new and different. By total cost of ownership, we mean the total of **capital expenditures (CAPEX)** in the form of equipment, and **operational expenditures (OPEX)** in the form of IT storage administrators, electricity, power, cooling, and so on. This TCO reduction must be achieved without sacrificing durability (keeping data intact) or availability.

Unlimited scalability

Whether the cloud storage offering is public, that is, offered by a service provider or it is private, that is, offered by central IT, it must have unlimited scalability. As we will see, cloud storage is built on distributed systems, meaning that it scales very well. Traditional storage systems typically have an upper limit, so this is a huge benefit.

Elastic

Storage virtualization decouples and abstracts the storage pool from its physical implementation. This means that you can get an elastic (grow and shrink as required) and unified storage pool, when in reality the underlying hardware is neither. IT professionals who have spent endless hours forecasting data growth and then waiting for their equipment will appreciate the magnitude of this benefit.

On-demand

Consumers do not reserve blocks of electricity and pay for it upfront in countries such as the United States. Yet we routinely pay for storage upfront whether we use it or not. Cloud storage uses a pay-as-you-go model, where you only pay for the data stored and the data accessed. This can result in huge cost savings for the storage user.

Universal access

The existing enterprise storage has limitations in terms of access. Block storage is very limiting; a server has to be on the same storage-area network, and LUNs (storage pools) cannot be shared. Network-attached-storage (NAS) must be *mounted* to access it. This creates limitations on the number of clients and requires LAN access. Cloud storage is extremely flexible — there is no limit on the number of users or from where you access it. This is possible since cloud storage systems usually use a REST API over HTTP (get, put, post, and delete) instead of traditional SCSI or CIFS/ NFS protocols.

Multitenanancy

This is both a benefit and a potential limitation. Cloud storage is typically multitenant. Tenants may be different organizations in a public cloud or different departments in a private cloud. The benefit is centralized management that reduces costs. On the other hand, security is *not* a real concern because of strong authentication, access controls, and various encryption options; but it is certainly a perceived issue.

Use cases

Storage systems have struggled to balance reliability, cost, and performance. Generally, you can get two out of the three mentioned aspects. Cloud storage optimizes reliability and cost, but not performance. In fact, as we will see later, reliability in cloud storage is better than traditional RAID when you reach a large scale. The way RAID works, you are at a very high risk of having a failure during a RAID rebuild. Cloud storage uses different techniques such as replication or erasure coding to provide high reliability even when scaled.

This means cloud storage is good for primary storage for applications such as web servers and application servers, but not for databases or high-performance computing tier 2/3 storage, for example, backup, archival (photos, documents, videos, logs, and so on), and creating an additional copy for disaster recovery.

Application impact

Cloud storage affects applications in two ways, its interface to storage and its behavior. First, applications need to port to a new and different storage interface. Second, applications need to handle an eventually consistent storage system. The second part requires explanation. Cloud storage is built using distributed systems, and it is based on a theorem called the CAP theorem, which states that out of the following three points, it is impossible to guarantee more than two:

- **Consistency**: For cloud storage, this means that a request to any region/node returns the same data
- **Availability**: For cloud storage, this signifies that a request is successfully acknowledged with a response
- **Partial tolerance**: For cloud storage, this implies that the architecture is able to withstand failures in connectivity or parts of the system

Most cloud storage systems guarantee availability and partial tolerance at the expense of consistency, making the system eventually consistent. This means that an operation such as write or delete may not be reflected to all nodes at the same time. Traditional applications expect strict consistency and must be modified.

Cloud gateways

If an application has not ported to cloud storage, is that a dead end? Fortunately not; there is a class of devices called cloud gateways that provide file or block interfaces to an application (for example, CIFS, NFS, iSCSI, or FTP/ SFTP) and perform protocol conversion to the cloud. These gateways provide other functionalities such as caching, WAN optimization, optional compression, encryption, and deduplication as well. These gateways also eliminate the need for an application to handle the eventual consistency problem.

Object storage

How do you build a cloud storage system? The most suitable underlying technology is object storage.

Object storage is different from block or file storage and it allows a user to store data in the form of objects (essentially files) in a flat namespace using REST HTTP APIs. Object storage completely virtualizes the physical implementation from the logical presentation. It is similar to check-in luggage versus carry-on luggage, where once you put your check-in luggage in the system, you really don't know where it is. You simply get it back at your destination. With carry-on luggage, you have to know exactly where you have kept it at all times.

Object storage is built using scale-out distributed systems. Each node, most often, actually runs on a local file system. As we will see, object storage architectures allow for the use of commodity hardware as opposed to expensive specialized hardware used by traditional storage systems. You could argue that object storage is a higher-level storage system than file systems. The two most critical tasks of an object storage system are:

- Data placement
- Automating management tasks

Typically, a user sends their HTTP GET, PUT, POST, or DELETE request to any one of a set of nodes, and the request is translated to physical nodes by the object storage software. The software also takes care of the durability model by either creating multiple copies of the object, chunking it, creating erasure codes, or a combination. The durability model is not RAID because RAID simply does not scale beyond hundreds of terabytes. The second critical task deals with management, such as periodic health checks, self-healing, and data migration. Management is also made easy by having a single flat namespace, which means that a storage administrator can manage the entire cluster as a single entity.

Let's evaluate, through the following table, how object storage meets the mentioned cloud storage benefits:

Criteria	Ability to meet
Low TCO	Storage nodes have no special requirements such as high availability, management, or special hardware such as RAID; this means commodity hardware can be used to cut capital expenses (CAPEX).
	A single flat namespace with automated management features allows you to cut operational expenses (OPEX).
	A full analysis of how this cuts the TCO by 10 times or more is outside the scope of this book.
Unlimited scalability	A distributed architecture allows capacity and performance to scale.
Elasticity	A fully virtualized approach allows data to grow and shrink as necessary.
On-demand	A fully virtualized approach with centralized management allows storage to be offered as an on-demand service.
Universal access	REST HTTP APIs provide access from wherever the user is, with no restriction on the number of users.
Multitenancy	A combination of multiple accounts, strong authentication, and access controls ensures multitenancy with adequate security.

OpenStack Swift

Is there an object storage stack best suited for our purposes? We believe the right choice is **OpenStack Swift**. Let us first look at what the OpenStack project is about, what OpenStack Swift (also referred to as just Swift) is, and then answer the preceding question about its choice.

OpenStack, a project launched by NASA and RackSpace in 2010, is currently the fastest growing open source project, and its mission is to produce a cloud computing platform useful for both public and private implementations. The two core principles are simplicity and scalability. OpenStack has numerous subprojects in its umbrella, ranging from computing and storing to networking, among others. The object storage project is called Swift and is a highly available, distributed, masterless, and eventually consistent software stack.

Why Swift when there are several vendors selling proprietary object storage software? The answer is in the first few sentences of this chapter; if you want to be like the web giants, the only option is open source. Open source cuts the total cost of ownership dramatically and provides access to a vibrant community that can provide technical support. Open source projects also provide longevity since open source has been shown to outlast proprietary projects. Moreover, open source projects allow users to benefit from the work done by bigger players and creates an ecosystem of tools and know-how. Finally, open source projects add functionality at a lot faster rate than proprietary projects. All this makes Swift the right choice.

The Swift project, in particular, came out of RackSpace's Cloud Files platform. The project was unique because the engineers and dev ops folks worked together to create it. This resulted in a very powerful storage system that is simple yet easy to manage. RackSpace "open-sourced" Swift in 2010 and numerous organizations such as Seagate, EVault, IBM, HP, Internap, Korea Telecom, Intel, SwiftStack, CloudScaling, Mirantis, and so on have joined the project since then.

In addition to sharing the mentioned generic object storage characteristics, OpenStack Swift has some unique additional functionality, as follows:

- **Open source**: With no license fees, as mentioned previously.
- **Open standards**: Using HTTP REST APIs with SSL for optional encryption. The combination of open source and open standards eliminates any potential vendor lock-in.

- **Account / container / object structure**: OpenStack Swift incorporates rich naming and organization capacity, unlike a number of object storage systems that offer a primitive interface where the user gets a key upon submitting an object. The burden of mapping names to keys and organizing them in a reasonable manner is left to the user.

- **Global cluster capability**: This allows replication and distribution of data around the world. This functionality helps with disaster recovery, distribution of hot data, and so on.

- **Partial object retrieval**: For example, if you want just a portion of a movie object or a TAR file.

- **Middleware architecture**: Allows you to add functionality. A great example of this is integrating with an authentication system.

- **Large object support**: For objects over 5 GB.

- **Additional functionality**: This includes object versioning, expiring objects, rate limiting, temporary URL support, CNAME lookup, domain remap, and static web mode. This list is constantly growing as a consequence of Swift being an open source project.

Summary

In this chapter, we covered why cloud storage is a new way to build storage systems that cuts the total cost of ownership significantly. It uses a technology called object storage. A high-quality open source object storage software stack to consider is OpenStack Swift. OpenStack Swift uses a dramatically different architecture than traditional enterprise storage systems by using a distributed architecture on commodity servers. The next chapter explains this architecture in detail.

2
OpenStack Swift Architecture

OpenStack Swift is the magic that converts a set of unconnected commodity servers into a scalable, durable, easy-to-manage storage system. We will look at Swift's architecture (Havana release) in detail. First, we will look at the logical organization of objects and then how Swift completely virtualizes this view and maps it to the physical hardware.

 Note that we will use the terms **durable** and **reliable** synonymously.

The logical organization of objects

First, let us look at the logical organization of objects and then how Swift completely abstracts and maps objects to the physical hardware.

A **tenant** is assigned an account. A tenant could be any entity — a person, a department, a company, and so on. The account holds containers. Each container holds objects, as shown in the following figure. You can think of objects essentially as files.

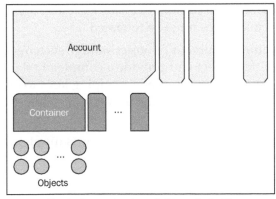

Logical organization of objects in Swift

A tenant can create additional **users** to access an account. Users can keep adding containers and objects within a container without having to worry about any physical hardware boundaries, unlike traditional file or block storage. Containers within an account obviously have to have a unique name, but two containers in separate accounts can have the same name. Containers are flat and objects are not stored hierarchically, unlike files stored in a filesystem where directories can be nested. However, Swift does provide a mechanism to simulate **pseudo-directories** by inserting a / delimiter in the object name.

The Swift implementation

The two key issues Swift has to solve are as follows:

- Where to put and fetch data
- How to keep the data reliable

We will explore the following topics to fully understand these two issues.

Key architectural principles

Some key architectural principles behind Swift are as follows:

- **Masterless**: A master in a system creates both a failure point and a performance bottleneck. Masterless removes this and also allows multiple members of the cluster to respond to API requests.

- **Loosely coupled**: There is no need for tight communication in the cluster. This is also essential to prevent performance and failure bottlenecks.

- **Load spreading**: Unless the load is spread out, performance, capacity, account, container, and object scalability cannot be achieved.

- **Self-healing**: The system must automatically adjust for hardware failures. As per the CAP theorem discussion in *Chapter 1, Cloud Storage: Why Can't I be like Google?* partial tolerances must be tolerated.

- **Data organization**: A number of object storage systems simply return a hash key for a submitted object and provide a completely flat namespace. The task of creating accounts, containers, and mapping keys to object names is left to the user. Swift simplifies life for the user and provides a well-designed data organization layer.

- **Available and eventually consistent**: This was discussed in *Chapter 1, Cloud Storage: Why Can't I be like Google?*.

Physical data organization

Swift completely abstracts logical organization of data from the physical organization. At a physical level, Swift classifies the physical location into a hierarchy, as shown in the following figure:

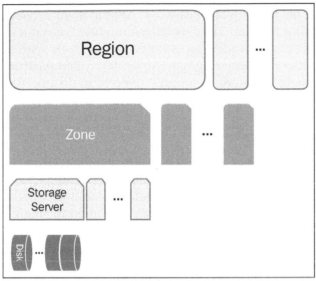

Physical data location hierarchy

- The hierarchy is as follows: **Region**: At the highest level, Swift stores data in regions that are geographically separated and thus suffer from a high-latency link. A user may use only one region, for example, if the cluster utilizes only one datacenter.

- **Zone**: Within regions, there are zones. Zones are a set of storage nodes that share different availability characteristics. Availability may be defined as different physical buildings, power sources, or network connections. This means that a zone could be a single storage server, a rack, or a complete datacenter depending on your requirements. Zones need to be connected to each other via low-latency links. Rackspace recommends having at least five zones per region.

- **Storage servers**: A zone consists of a set of storage servers ranging from just one to several racks.

- **Disk** (or devices): Disk drives are part of a storage server. These could be inside the server or connected via a JBOD.

Swift will store a number of **replicas** (default = 3) of an object onto different disks. Using an as-unique-as-possible algorithm, these replicas are as "far" away as possible in terms of being in different regions, zones, storage servers, and disks. This algorithm is responsible for the durability aspect of Swift.

Swift uses a semi-static table to look up where to place objects and their replicas. It is semi-static because the look-up table called a "ring" in Swift is created by an external process called the **ring builder**. The ring can be modified, but not dynamically; and never by Swift. It is not distributed, so every node that deals with data placement has a complete copy of the ring. The ring has entries in it called **partitions** (this term is not to be confused with the more commonly referred to disk partitions). Essentially, an object is mapped to a partition, and the partition provides the devices where the replicas of an object are to be stored. The ring also provides a list of handoff devices should any of the initial ones fail.

The actual storage of the object is done on a filesystem that resides on the disk, for example, XFS. Account and container information is kept in SQLite databases. The account database contains a list of all its containers, and the container database contains a list of all its objects. These databases are stored in single files, and the files are replicated just like any other object.

Data path software servers

The data path consists of the following four software servers:

- Proxy server
- Account server
- Container server
- Object server

Unless you need performance, then account, container, and object servers are often put on one physical server and called a **storage server** (or node), as shown in the following figure:

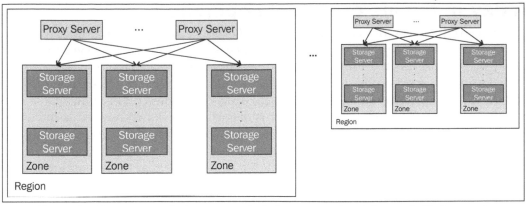

Data path software servers (a storage server includes an account, container, and object servers)

- A description of each server type is as follows: **Proxy server**: The proxy server is responsible for accepting HTTP requests from a user. It will look up the location of the storage server(s) where the request needs to be routed by utilizing the ring. The proxy server accounts for failures (by looking up handoff nodes) and performs read/write affinity (by sending writes or reads to the same region; Refer to *A day in the life of a create operation* and *A day in the life of a read operation* sections). When objects are streamed to or from an object server, they are streamed directly through the proxy server as well. Moreover, proxy servers are also responsible for the read/write quorum and often host inline middleware (discussed later in this chapter).

- **Account server**: The account server tracks the names of containers in a particular account. Data is stored in SQLite databases; database files are further stored on the filesystem. This server also tracks statistics, but does not have any location information about containers. The location information is determined by the proxy server based on the ring. Normally, this server is hosted on the same physical server with container and object servers. However, in large installations, this may need to be on a separate physical server.

- **Container server**: This server is very similar to the account server, except that it deals with object names in a particular container.

- **Object server**: Object servers simply store objects. Each disk has a filesystem on it, and objects are stored in those filesystems.

Let us stitch the physical organization of the data with the various software components and explore the four basic operations: create, read, update, and delete (known as CRUD). For simplicity, we are focusing on the object server, but it may be further extrapolated to both account and container servers too.

A day in the life of a create operation

A create request is sent via an HTTP PUT API call to a proxy server. It does not matter which proxy server gets the request since Swift is a distributed system and all proxy servers are created equal. The proxy server interacts with the ring to get a list of disks and associated object servers to write data to. As we covered earlier, these disks will be as unique as possible. If certain disks have failed or are unavailable, the ring provides handoff devices. Once the majority of disks acknowledge the write (for example, two out of three disks), the operation is returned as being successful. Assuming the remaining writes complete successfully, we are fine. If not, the replication process, shown in the following figure, ensures that the remaining copies are ultimately created:

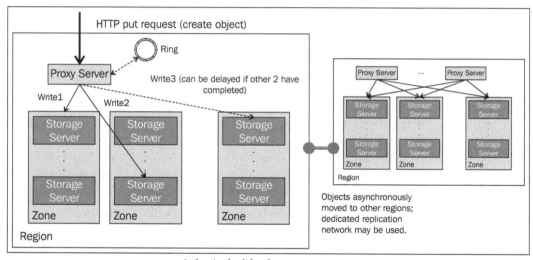

A day in the life of a create operation

The create operation operation works slightly differently in a multiregion cluster. All copies of the object are written to the local region. This is called **write affinity**. The object is then asynchronously moved to other region(s). A dedicated replication network may be used for this operation.

A day in the life of a read operation

A read request is sent via an HTTP GET API call to a proxy server. Again, any proxy server can receive this request. Similar to the create operation, the proxy server interacts with the ring to get a list of disks and associated object servers. The read request is issued to object servers in the same region as the proxy server. This is called read affinity. For a multiregion implementation, eventual consistency presents a problem since different regions might have different versions of an object. To get around this issue, a read for an object with the latest timestamp may be requested. In this case, proxy servers first request the time stamp from all the object servers and read from the server with the newest copy. Similar to the write case, in the case of a failure, handoff devices may be requested.

A day in the life of an update operation

An update request is handled in the same manner as a write request. Objects are stored with their timestamp to make sure that when read, the latest version of the object is returned. Swift also supports a versioning feature on a per-container basis. When this is turned on, older versions of the object are also available in a special container called versions_container.

A day in the life of a delete operation

A delete request sent via an HTTP DELETE API call is treated like an update but instead of a new version, a "tombstone" version with zero bytes is placed. The delete operation is very difficult in a distributed system since the system will essentially fight a delete by recreating deleted copies. The Swift solution is indeed very elegant and eliminates the possibility of deleted objects suddenly showing up again.

Postprocessing software components

There are three key postprocessing software components that run in the background, as opposed to being part of the data path.

Replication

Replication is a very important aspect of Swift. Replication ensures that the system is consistent, that is, all servers and disks assigned by the ring to hold copies of an object or database do indeed have the latest version. The process protects against failures, hardware migration, and ring rebalancing (where the ring is changed and data has to be moved around). This is done by comparing local data with the remote copy. If the remote copy needs to be updated, the replication process "pushes" a copy. The comparison process is pretty efficient and is carried out by simply comparing hash lists rather than comparing each byte of an object (or account or container database). Replication uses `rsync`, a Linux based remote file synchronization utility, to copy data but there are plans to replace it with a faster mechanism.

Updaters

In certain situations, account or container servers may be busy due to heavy load or being unavailable. In this case, the update is queued onto the storage server's local storage. There are two **updaters** to process these queued items. The object updater will update objects in the container database while the container updater will update containers in the account database. This situation could lead to an interesting eventual consistency behavior where the object is available, but the container listing does not have it at that time. These windows of inconsistency are generally very small.

Auditors

Auditors walk through every object, container, and account to check their data integrity. This is done by computing an MD5 hash and comparing it to the stored hash. If the item is found corrupted, it is moved to a quarantine directory and in time, the replication process will create a clean copy. This is how the system is self-healing. The MD5 hash is also available to the user so they can perform operations such as comparing the hash of their location object with the one stored on Swift.

Other processes

The other background processes are as follows:

- **Account reaper**: This process runs in the background and is responsible for deleting an entire account once it is marked for deletion in the database.
- **Object expirer**: Swift allows users to set retention policies by providing "delete-at" or "delete-after" information for objects. This process ensures that expired objects are deleted.

- **Drive audit**: This is another useful background process that looks out for bad drives and unmounts them. This can be more efficient than letting the auditor deal with this failure.

- **Container to container synchronization**: Finally using the container to container synchronization process, all contents of a container to be mirrored to another container. These containers can be in different clusters and the operation uses a secret sync key. Before multiregion support, this feature was the only way to get multiple copies of your data in two or more regions, and thus this feature is less important now than before. However, it is still very useful for hybrid (private-public combination) or community clouds (multiple private clouds).

Inline middleware options

In addition to the mentioned core data path components, other items may also be placed in the data path to extend Swift functionality. This is done by taking advantage of Swift's architecture, which allows middleware to be inserted. The following is a non-exhaustive list of various middleware modules. Most of them apply only to the proxy server, while some modules such as logging and recon do apply to other servers as well.

Auth

Authentication is one of the most important inline functions. All Swift middleware is separate and is used to extend Swift; thus auth systems are separate projects and one of several may be chosen. Keystone auth is the official OpenStack identity service and may be used in conjunction with Swift, though there is nothing to prevent a user from creating their own auth system or using others such as Swauth or TempAuth.

Authentication works as follows:

1. A user presents credentials to the auth system. This is done by executing an HTTP REST API call.

2. The auth system provides the user with an AUTH token.

3. The AUTH token is not unique for every request, but expires after a certain duration.

4. Every request made to Swift has to be accompanied by the AUTH token.

5. Swift validates the token with the Auth system and caches the result. The result is flushed upon expiration.

6. The Auth system generally has the concept of administrator accounts and non-admin accounts. Administrator requests are obviously passed through.

7. Non-admin requests are checked against container level **Access Control Lists** (**ACL**). These lists allow the administrator to set read and write ACLs for each non-admin user.

8. Therefore, for non-admin users, the ACL is checked before the proxy server proceeds with the request. The following figure illustrates the steps involved when Swift interacts with the Auth system:

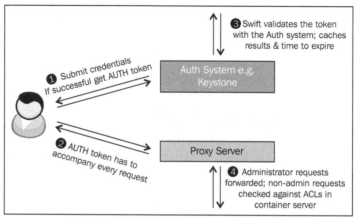

Swift and its interaction with the Auth system

Logging

Logging is a very important module. This middleware provides logging. A user may insert their custom log handler as well.

Other modules

A number of other Swift and third-party middleware modules are available; the following are a few examples:

- **Health check**: This module provides a simple way to monitor if the proxy server is alive. Simply access the proxy server with the path / health check and the server will respond with OK.

- **Domain remap**: This middleware allows you to remap the account and container name from the path into the host domain name. This allows you to simplify domain names.

- **CNAME lookup**: Using this software, you can create friendly domain names that remap directly to your account or container. CNAME lookup and domain remap may be used in conjunction.

- **Rate limiting**: Rate limiting is used to limit the rate of requests that result in database writes to account and container servers.

- **Container and account quotas**: An administrator can set container or account quotas by using these two middleware modules.

- **Bulk delete**: This middleware allows bulk operations such as deletion of multiple objects or containers.

- **Bulk archive auto-extraction**: For bulk expansion of TAR (TAR, `tar.gz`, `tar.bz2`) files to be performed with a single command, use this software.

- **TempURL**: The TempURL middleware allows you to create a URL that provides temporary access to an object. This access is not authenticated but expires after a certain duration of time. Furthermore, the access is only to a single object and no other objects can be accessed via the URL.

- **Swift origin server**: This is a module that allows the use of Swift as an origin server to a **Content Delivery Network (CDN)**.

- **Static web**: This software converts Swift into a static web server. You can also provide CSS stylesheets to get full control over the look and feel of your pages. Obviously, requests can be from anonymous sources.

- **Form post**: Using the form post middleware, you get the ability to upload objects to Swift using standard HTML form posts. The middleware converts the different POST requests to different PUT requests, and the requests do not go through authentication to allow collaboration across users and non-users of the cluster.

- **Recon**: Recon is software useful for management. It provides monitoring and returns various metrics about the cluster.

Additional features

Swift has additional features not covered in the previous sections. The following sections detail some of the additional features.

Large object support

Swift places a limit on the size of a single uploaded object (default is 5 GB), yet allows for the storage and downloading of virtually unlimited size objects. The technique used is segmentation. An object is broken up into equal-size segments (except the last one) and uploaded. These uploads are efficient since no one segment is unreasonably large and data transfers can be done in parallel. Once uploads are complete, a manifest file, which shows how the segments form one single large object, is uploaded. The download is a single operation where Swift concatenates the various segments to recreate the single large object.

Metadata

Swift allows custom metadata to be attached to accounts, containers, or objects that are set and retrieved in the form of custom headers. The metadata is simply a key (name) value pair. Metadata may be provided at the time of creating an object (using PUT) or updated later (using POST). Metadata may be retrieved independently of the object by using the HEAD method.

Multirange support

The HTTP specification allows for a multirange GET operation, and Swift supports this by retrieving multiple ranges of an object rather than the entire object.

CORS

CORS is a specification that allows JavaScript running in a browser to make a request to domains other than where it came from. Swift supports this, and this feature makes it possible for you to host your web pages with JavaScript on one domain and request objects from a Swift cluster on another domain. Swift also supports a broader cross-domain policy file where other client-side technologies such as Flash, Java, and Silverlight can also interact with Swift that is in a different domain.

Server-side copies

Swift allows you to make a copy of an object using a different container location and/or object name. The entire copy operation is performed on the server side, thus offloading the client.

Cluster health

A tool called swift-dispersion-report may be used to measure the overall cluster health. It does so by ensuring that the various replicas of an object and container are in their proper places.

Summary

In summary, Swift takes a set of commodity servers and creates a reliable and scalable storage system that is simple to manage. In this chapter, we reviewed the Swift architecture and major functionalities. The next chapter shows how you can install Swift on your own environment using multiple servers.

3
Installing OpenStack Swift

The previous chapter should have given you a good understanding of OpenStack Swift's architecture. Now, let's delve into the installation details of OpenStack Swift. This chapter is meant for IT administrators who want to install OpenStack Swift. The version discussed here is the Havana release of OpenStack. Installation of Swift has several steps and requires careful planning before beginning the process. A simple installation consists of installing all the Swift components in one node, and a complex installation consists of installing Swift on several proxy server nodes and storage server nodes. The number of storage nodes can be in the order of thousands across multiple zones and regions. Depending on your installation, you need to decide on the number of proxy server nodes and storage server nodes that you will configure. This chapter demonstrates a manual installation process; advanced users may want to use utilities such as Puppet or Chef to simplify the process.

This chapter walks you through an OpenStack Swift cluster installation that contains one proxy server and five storage servers. As explained in *Chapter 2, OpenStack Swift Architecture*, storage servers include account, container, and object servers.

Hardware planning

This section describes the various hardware components involved in the setup (see *Chapter 6, Choosing the Right Hardware*, for a complete discussion on this topic). Since Swift deals with object storage, disks are going to be a big part of hardware planning. The size and number of disks required should be calculated based on your requirements. Networking is also an important component where factors such as public/private network and a separate network for communication between storage servers need to be planned. Network throughput of at least 1Gbps is suggested, while 10 Gbps is recommended.

The servers we set up as proxy and storage servers are dual quad-core servers with 12 GB of RAM.

In our setup, we have a total of 15 x 2 TB disks for Swift storage; this gives us a total size of 30 TB. However, with in-built replication (with default replica count of 3), Swift maintains three copies of the same data, and hence, the effective storage capacity for storing files/objects is 10 TB. This is further reduced due to less than 100 percent utilization. The following figure depicts the nodes of our Swift cluster configuration:

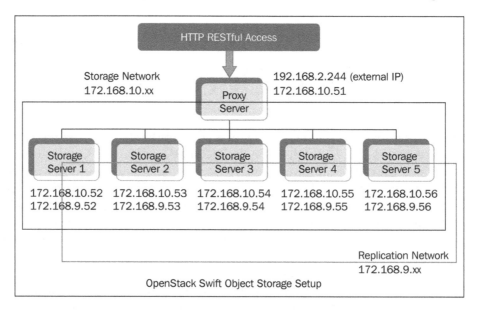

Server setup and network configuration

All the servers are installed with the Ubuntu operating system (Version 12.04).

You need to configure three networks, which are as follows:

- **Public network**: The proxy server connects to this network. This network provides public access to the API endpoints within the proxy server.

- **Storage network**: This is a private network not accessible to the outside world. All the storage servers and the proxy server will connect to this network. Communication between the proxy server and the storage servers, and communication between the storage servers, takes place within this network. In our configuration, the IP addresses assigned in this network are 172.168.10.0/172.168.10.99.

- **Replication network**: This also is a private network that is not accessible to the outside world. It is dedicated to replication traffic, and only storage servers connect to this network. All replication-related communication between storage servers takes place within this network. In our configuration, the IP addresses assigned in this network are 172.168.9.0 / 172.168.9.99.

Preinstallation steps

In order for the various servers to communicate easily, edit the /etc/hosts file, and add the hostnames of each server in it. This is performed on all the nodes. The following image shows an example of the contents of the /etc/hosts file of the proxy server node:

```
127.0.0.1          localhost
192.168.2.244      swift-proxy
172.168.10.51      s-swift-proxy
172.168.10.52      swift-storage1
172.168.10.53      swift-storage2
172.168.10.54      swift-storage3
172.168.10.55      swift-storage4
172.168.10.56      swift-storage5
```

Install the NTP service on the proxy server node and storage server nodes. This helps all the nodes in synchronizing their services effectively without any clock delays. The pre-installation steps to be performed are as follows:

1. Configure the proxy server node to be the reference server for the storage server nodes to set their time from the proxy server node:

```
# apt-get install ntp
```

2. Add the following line to /etc/ntp.conf for NTP configuration in the proxy server node:

   server ntp.ubuntu.com

3. For NTP configuration in storage server nodes, add the following line to /etc/ntp.conf. Comment out the remaining lines with server addresses such as 0.ubuntu.pool.ntp.org, 1.ubuntu.pool.ntp.org, 2.ubuntu.pool.ntp.org, and 3.ubuntu.pool.ntp.org:

   server s-swift-proxy

4. Restart the NTP service on each server with the following command:

```
# service ntp restart
```

Downloading and installing Swift

The Ubuntu Cloud archive is a special repository that provides users with the capability to install new releases of OpenStack.

The steps to perform to download and install Swift are as follows:

1. Enable the capability to install new releases of OpenStack and install the latest version of Swift on each node using the following commands:

```
# apt-get install python-software-properties
# add-apt-repository cloud-archive:havana
```

2. Now, update the OS using the following command:

```
# apt-get update && apt-get dist-upgrade
```

3. On all the Swift nodes, we will install the prerequisite software and services using the following command:

```
# apt-get install swift rsync memcached python-netifaces
python-xattr python-memcache
```

4. Next, we create a Swift folder under /etc and give the user permission to access this folder by using the following commands:

```
# mkdir -p /etc/swift
# chown -R swift:swift /etc/swift
```

5. Create a /etc/swift/swift.conf file and add a variable called swift_hash_path_suffix in the swift-hash section. We then create a unique hash string using Python -c "from uuid import uuid4; print uuid4()" or openssl rand -hex 10 and assign it to this variable as shown in the following command:

```
[swift-hash]
# random unique string that can never change (DO NOT LOSE)
swift_hash_path_suffix = sLSDQfffedFUHIjjakM
```

6. We then add another variable called `swift_hash_path_prefix` to the `swift-hash` section and assign another hash string created using the method described in the preceding step to it. These strings will be used in the hashing process to determine the mappings in the ring. The `swift.conf` file should be identical on all the nodes in the cluster.

Setting up storage server nodes

This section explains additional steps to set up the storage server node.

Installing services

On each storage server node, install the swift-account, swift-container, swift-object, and xfsprogs(XFS Filesystem) packages using the following command:

```
# apt-get install swift-account swift-container swift-object xfsprogs
```

Formatting and mounting hard disks

On each storage server node, we need to identify the hard disks that will be used to store the data. We will then format the hard disks and mount them to a directory, which Swift will then use to store data. We will not create any RAID levels or any subpartitions on these hard disks because they are not necessary for Swift. They will be used as whole disks. The operating system will be installed on separate disks, which will be RAID-configured.

First, identify the hard disks that are going to be used for storage, and format them. In our storage server, we have identified **sdb**, **sdc**, and **sdd**, which will be used for storage.

We will perform the following four operations on **sdb**. These four steps should be repeated for **sdc** and **sdd** as well:

1. Do the partitioning for **sdb** and create the filesystem using the following command.

```
# fdisk /dev/sdb
# mkfs.xfs /dev/sdb1
```

2. Then, let's create a directory in /srv/node that will be used to mount the filesystem. Give permission to the swift user to be able to access this directory. These operations can be performed by using the following commands:

```
# mkdir -p /srv/node/sdb1
# chown -R swift:swift /srv/node
```

3. We set up an entry in **fstab** for the **sdb1** partition in the **sdb** hard disk, as follows. This will automatically mount **sdb1** to /srv/node/sdb1 on every boot. Add the following command line to /etc/fstab file:

```
/dev/sdb1 /srv/node/sdb1 xfs noatime,nodiratime,nobarrier,logbufs=8 0 0
```

4. Mount **sdb1** to /srv/node/sdb1 by using the following command:

```
# mount /srv/node/sdb1
```

RSYNC and RSYNCD

In order for Swift to perform replication of data, we need to set up rsync and rsyncd.conf by performing the following steps:

1. Create the rsyncd.conf file in the /etc folder with the following content:

```
# vi /etc/rsyncd.conf
```

```
uid = swift
gid = swift
log file = /var/log/rsyncd.log
pid file = /var/run/rsyncd.pid
address = 172.168.9.52
[account]
max connections = 2
path = /srv/node/
read only = false
lock file = /var/lock/account.lock
[container]
max connections = 2
path = /srv/node/
read only = false
lock file = /var/lock/container.lock
[object]
max connections = 2
path = /srv/node/
read only = false
lock file = /var/lock/object.lock
```

172.168.9.52 is the IP address that is on the replication network for this storage server. Use the appropriate replication network IP addresses for the corresponding storage servers.

2. We then have to edit the /etc/default/rsync file and set RSYNC_ENABLE to true using the following command:

```
RSYNC_ENABLE=true
```

3. We then have to restart the rsync service by using the following command:

```
# service rsync start
```

4. Next, we create the swift recon cache directory by using the following command, and then set its permissions:

```
# mkdir -p /var/swift/recon
```

Setting permissions is done using the following command:

```
# chown -R swift:swift /var/swift/recon
```

Repeat these steps on every storage server.

Setting up the proxy server node

This section explains the steps to set up the proxy server node, which are as follows:

1. Install the following services only on the proxy server node:

```
# apt-get install swift-proxy memcached python-keystoneclient
python-swiftclient python-webob
```

 Openssl has already been installed as part of the operating system installation to support HTTPS.

2. We are going to use the OpenStack Keystone service for authentication. So, we have to create the `proxy-server.conf` file and add the following content to it:

```
# vi /etc/swift/proxy-server.conf
```

Add the following configuration information to the `proxy-server.conf` file:

```
[DEFAULT]
bind_port = 8888
user = swift
[pipeline:main]
pipeline = healthcheck cache authtoken keystoneauth proxy-server
[app:proxy-server]
use = egg:swift#proxy
allow_account_management = true
account_autocreate = true
[filter:keystoneauth]
use = egg:swift#keystoneauth
operator_roles = Member,admin,swiftoperator
[filter:authtoken]
paste.filter_factory = keystoneclient.middleware.auth_token:filter_factory
# Delaying the auth decision is required to support token-less
# usage for anonymous referrers ('.r:*').
delay_auth_decision = true
# cache directory for signing certificate
signing_dir = /home/swift/keystone-signing
# auth_* settings refer to the Keystone server
auth_protocol = http
# the hostname of the proxy server
auth_host = swift-proxy
auth_port = 35357
# the same admin_token as provided in keystone.conf
admin_token = Random Token
# the service tenant and swift userid and password created in Keystone
admin_tenant_name = admin
admin_user = admin
admin_password = vedadms123
[filter:cache]
use = egg:swift#memcache
[filter:catch_errors]
use = egg:swift#catch_errors
```

3. The `proxy-server.conf` file should be edited to have the correct `auth_host`, `admin_token`, `admin_tenant_name`, `admin_user`, and `admin_password` (refer to the following keystone setup section to see how to set up the correct credentials).

4. Next, we create a `keystone-signing` directory and give permissions to the `swift` user using the following commands:

```
# mkdir -p /home/swift/keystone-signing
# chown -R swift:swift /home/swift/keystone-signing
```

The ring setup

As discussed in *Chapter 2, OpenStack Swift Architecture*, the ring (also called ring builder, or simply builder file) contains information to map the user API request information to the physical location of the account, container, or object. We will have a builder file for accounts, which will contain mapping information for the account. Similarly, we will have a builder file for containers and objects.

Builder files are created using the following commands:

```
# cd /etc/swift
# swift-ring-builder account.builder create 18 3 1
# swift-ring-builder container.builder create 18 3 1
# swift-ring-builder object.builder create 18 3 1
```

The parameter 18 indicates that there can be 2 to the power of 18 partitions created to store the data. To determine the number of partitions, estimate the maximum number of disks, multiply that number by 100, and then round it up to the nearest power of two. Picking a number smaller than needed is not catastrophic; it will just result in an unbalanced cluster from a storage capacity point of view. Picking a number larger than needed will impact performance. The parameter 3 indicates that three replicas of data will be stored, and the parameter 1 is set in such a way that we don't move a partition more than once in an hour.

In Swift storage, hard disks can be grouped into zones, and rings can be set up according to the zones. Each hard disk in a storage server belongs to a particular zone. This helps Swift replicate the data to different zones in an as-unique-as-possible manner. If there is a failure in a particular zone, data can be fetched from the data copies in other zones. In a multiregion setup, if there is a failure in a particular region, then data can be fetched from other regions.

The following command syntax is used to add storage server hard disk devices to ring builder files. Please note that the region and zone the hard disk belongs to is provided as an input parameter. The weight parameter (100) indicates how much data is going to be placed on this disk compared to other disks.

Run the following commands to add the hard disks allocated for storage to the ring. In order to add mapping for the **sdb1** device, we run the following commands:

```
# swift-ring-builder account.builder add r1z1-172.168.10.52:6002\
R172.168.9.52:6005/sdb1 100
# swift-ring-builder container.builder add r1z1-172.168.10.52:60\
01R172.168.9.52:6004/sdb1 100
# swift-ring-builder object.builder add r1z1-172.168.10.52:6000R\
172.168.9.52:6003/sdb1 100
```

In the preceding commands, `172.168.10.52` is the IP address of the storage node in the storage network that contains **sdb1**, and `172.168.9.52` is the IP address of the same storage node in the replication network.

We have to run the preceding commands by replacing **sdb1** with **sdc1** and **sdd1** for this storage network IP address and replication network IP address. We have to run the same commands to add **sdb1**, **sdc1**, and **sdd1** of the remaining storage servers as well by giving their storage network IP addresses and replication network IP addresses in the commands.

The final step in completing the ring builder process is creating the ring files that will be used by the Swift processes. This is done using the rebalance command, as shown:

```
# swift-ring-builder account.builder rebalance
# swift-ring-builder container.builder rebalance
# swift-ring-builder object.builder rebalance
```

Upon running the preceding commands, the following files will be created: `account.ring.gz`, `container.ring.gz`, and `object.ring.gz`. Copy these files into the `etc/swift` directory of all the nodes in the cluster.

Also, make sure that `/etc/swift` has `swift` user permissions on every node. Set up user permissions using the following command:

```
# chown -R swift:swift /etc/swift
```

Now we can start the proxy service as follows:

```
# service swift-proxy restart
```

Starting services on all storage nodes

Now that the storage servers have the ring files (`account.ring.gz`, `container.ring.gz`, and `object.ring.gz`), we can start the Swift services on the storage servers using the following commands:

```
# service swift-object start
# service swift-object-replicator start
# service swift-object-updater start
# service swift-object-auditor start
# service swift-container start
# service swift-container-replicator start
# service swift-container-updater start
# service swift-container-auditor start
# service swift-account start
# service swift-account-replicator start
# service swift-account-reaper start
# service swift-account-auditor start
```

We should also start the rsyslog and memcached services on the storage servers by using the following commands:

```
# service rsyslog restart
# service memcached restart
```

Multiregion support

In multiregion installation, we place a pool of storage nodes in one region and the remaining in other regions. We can either have a single endpoint for all the regions or a separate endpoint for each region. During the ring builder setup, the region is specified as a parameter. Clients can access any endpoint and do the operations (create, delete, and so on), and they will be replicated across other regions. The proxy server configuration files will contain read_affinity and write_affinity in a particular region.

Our test configuration had two proxy servers and five storage nodes. Two regions were created by creating two endpoints. A list of the endpoints gives the following output, which has been truncated for better readability:

```
# keystone endpoint-list
+------------------------------+--------------------+-------------
----------------------------------++
|id|    region         |     publicurl
|          adminurl         |
+------------------------------+--------------------+-------------
----------------------------------++
|  |  Swift-Region2    | http://192.168.2.231:8888/v1/AUTH_%(tenant_
id)s | http://192.168.2.231:8888/v1   |
```

```
|   |Openstack-Identity |            http://192.168.2.230:5000/v2.0
| http://192.168.2.230:35357/v2.0
|   |  Swift-Region1    | http://192.168.2.244:8888/v1/AUTH_%(tenant_
id)s | http://192.168.2.244:8888/v1  |
+-------------------------------+--------------------+-------------
-----------------------------------++
```

Swift-Region2 and Swift-Region1 are the two regions, and Openstack-Identity is the authentication endpoint.

The Keystone service

We will be using the Keystone service for authentication. The Keystone service exposes an endpoint that a user will connect to using username and tenant credentials. After validation by the Keystone identity service, a token that will be cached and used in further API calls to various other OpenStack API endpoints is returned to the user. Within Keystone, a user is defined to have account credentials and is associated with one or more tenants. Also, a user can be given a role such as admin (metadata information), which entitles this user to more privileges than an ordinary user.

Let us consider the case where a user is connecting to a Swift endpoint to read an object. When a user initiates an API call along with a token to the Swift endpoint, this token is passed by the Swift endpoint back to Keystone for validation. Once validated by Keystone, it returns a success code back to the Swift endpoint. The Swift service will then continue processing the API to read the object.

We now show the steps necessary to install and configure the Keystone service in the following sections.

Installing MySQL

We will use MySQL for the Keystone database. The installation steps are as follows.

1. Install the MySQL database and client software on the proxy server node by using the following command:

    root@swift-proxy:/home/vedams# apt-get install python-mysqldb mysql-server

2. Edit /etc/mysql/my.cnf in the proxy node, assigning the proxy server host name to Bind-address, as shown in following command:

    Bind-address = swift-proxy

3. Restart the MySQL service on the proxy node by using the following command:

```
root@swift-proxy:/home/vedams# service mysql restart
```

4. Delete anonymous users by using the `mysql_secure_installation` command, as follows:

```
root@swift-proxy:/home/vedams# mysql_secure_installation
```

5. Respond with `yes` to `delete anonymous user prompt`.

Installing Keystone

Keystone may be installed on dedicated servers for large installations, but for this example, install Keystone service on the proxy node. The following steps describe how to install and setup the Keystone service:

1. Install the Keystone service using the following command.

```
# apt-get install keystone
```

2. We have to generate a random token to access the Keystone service, as shown in the following command:

```
# openssl rand -hex 10
```

3. We then edit the `/etc/keystone/keystone.conf` file and perform the following changes:

   ° Replace `admin_token` with the random token that gets generated, as shown in the following command line:

   ```
   admin_token = Random Token
   ```

   ° Replace SQLite with a MySQL database connection using the following command:

```
connection = mysql://keystone:vedams123@swift-proxy/keystone
```

4. Make sure that the SQLite file has been deleted after configuring MySQL; otherwise, we need to manually delete the file. Run the following command to list the contents of the /var/lib/keystone directory and delete the keystone.sqlite file if present:

    #sudo ls -la /var/lib/keystone/

5. We then create the Keystone database user and grant permissions using the following commands:

```
root@swift-proxy:/home/vedams# mysql -u root -pvedams123
Welcome to the MySQL monitor.  Commands end with ; or \g.
Your MySQL connection id is 38
Server version: 5.5.34-0ubuntu0.12.04.1 (Ubuntu)

Copyright (c) 2000, 2013, Oracle and/or its affiliates. All rights reserved.

Oracle is a registered trademark of Oracle Corporation and/or its
affiliates. Other names may be trademarks of their respective
owners.

Type 'help;' or '\h' for help. Type '\c' to clear the current input statement.

mysql> CREATE DATABASE keystone;
Query OK, 1 row affected (0.00 sec)

mysql> GRANT ALL PRIVILEGES ON keystone.* TO 'keystone'@'localhost' IDENTIFIED BY 'vedams123';
Query OK, 0 rows affected (0.00 sec)

mysql> GRANT ALL PRIVILEGES ON keystone.* TO 'keystone'@'%' IDENTIFIED BY 'vedams123';
Query OK, 0 rows affected (0.00 sec)

mysql> quit
Bye
root@swift-proxy:/home/vedams#
```

6. Next, we check the Keystone database synchronization and restart the Keystone service by using the following commands:

```
# keystone-manage db_sync
# service keystone restart
```

7. Export the following environment variables:

```
# export OS_SERVICE_TOKEN=Random Token
# export OS_SERVICE_ENDPOINT=http://swift-proxy:35357/v2.0
```

8. We then set up a tenant, user, and role to authenticate the input credentials against. Once authenticated, access to Swift services and endpoints is permitted. We then create a tenant for an administrator user, an administrator user called admin, and a role for administrative tasks. We then add an admin role to the admin user. This is shown in the following command lines:

```
# keystone tenant-create --name=admin --description="Admin Tenant"
# keystone user-create --name=admin --pass=vedams123 --email=test@gmail.com
# keystone role-create --name=admin
# keystone user-role-add --user=admin --tenant=admin --role=admin
```

The following screenshot shows the output of executing the preceding commands:

```
root@swift-proxy:/home/vedams# keystone tenant-create --name=admin --description="Admin Tenant"
+-------------+----------------------------------+
|   Property  |              Value               |
+-------------+----------------------------------+
| description |           Admin Tenant           |
|   enabled   |               True               |
|     id      | f570de35b6dc4a4d81a24516d049173a |
|    name     |              admin               |
+-------------+----------------------------------+
root@swift-proxy:/home/vedams# keystone user-create --name=admin --pass=vedams123 --email=test@gmail.com
+----------+----------------------------------+
| Property |              Value               |
+----------+----------------------------------+
|  email   |          test@gmail.com          |
| enabled  |               True               |
|    id    | 77461f6a3763462b990cdaceec034afe |
|   name   |              admin               |
+----------+----------------------------------+
root@swift-proxy:/home/vedams# keystone role-create --name=admin
+----------+----------------------------------+
| Property |              Value               |
+----------+----------------------------------+
|    id    | 814ffeof0bbc4221a9ab98618d159ded |
|   name   |              admin               |
+----------+----------------------------------+
root@swift-proxy:/home/vedams# keystone user-role-add --user=admin --tenant=admin --role=admin
root@swift-proxy:/home/vedams# 
```

We then create another user called swift-user and add it to the tenant called swift-tenant. The user is given member access role. The following screenshot shows the creation process:

```
root@swift-proxy:/home/vedams# keystone tenant-create --name=swift-tenant --description="Swift Tenant"
+-------------+----------------------------------+
|   Property  |              Value               |
+-------------+----------------------------------+
| description |           Swift Tenant           |
|   enabled   |               True               |
|     id      | bd1e87f876e541a4acc42803430a1b2b |
|    name     |           swift-tenant           |
+-------------+----------------------------------+
root@swift-proxy:/home/vedams# keystone user-create --name=swift-user --pass=vedams123 --email=swiftuser@gmail.com
+----------+----------------------------------+
| Property |              Value               |
+----------+----------------------------------+
|  email   |        swiftuser@gmail.com        |
| enabled  |               True               |
|    id    | 0b81ddf04865444bbbdd4be417a392fc |
|   name   |            swift-user            |
+----------+----------------------------------+
root@swift-proxy:/home/vedams# keystone user-role-add --user=swift-user --tenant=swift-tenant --role=_member_
root@swift-proxy:/home/vedams#
```

9. The Keystone service keeps track of the various OpenStack services that we have installed and also keeps track of where they are in the network. In order to keep track of the services, IDs are created for the services using keystone **service-create** command as shown in the following commands:

```
# keystone service-create --name=keystone --type=identity \
--description="Keystone Identity Service"
# keystone service-create --name=swift --type=object-store \
--description="swift Service"
```

The following screenshot shows the output of executing the preceding service-create commands:

```
root@swift-proxy:/home/vedams# keystone service-create --name=keystone --type=identity --description="Keystone Identity Servi
ce"
+-------------+----------------------------------+
|  Property   |              Value               |
+-------------+----------------------------------+
| description |     Keystone Identity Service    |
|     id      | a9c2d44442464975bb50e296fcc584b4 |
|    name     |             keystone             |
|    type     |             identity             |
+-------------+----------------------------------+
root@swift-proxy:/home/vedams# keystone service-create --name=swift --type=object-store --description="Swift Object storage s
ervice"
+-------------+----------------------------------+
|  Property   |              Value               |
+-------------+----------------------------------+
| description |    Swift Object storage service  |
|     id      | a0ab378728b148fd9c9a0534d1d6a227 |
|    name     |              swift               |
|    type     |           object-store           |
+-------------+----------------------------------+
root@swift-proxy:/home/vedams#
```

10. We then need to specify the Keystone service endpoints and Swift service endpoints to Keystone using the `endpoint-create` command. In the following commands, `swift-proxy` is the hostname of the proxy server:

```
# keystone endpoint-create --service-id KEYSTONE_SERVICE_ID
--region RegionOne --publicurl 'http://swift-proxy:5000/v2.0'
--adminurl 'http://swift-proxy:35357/v2.0' --internalurl
'http://swift- proxy:5000/v2.0'
# keystone endpoint-create --service-id SWIFT_SERVICE_ID
--region regionOne
--publicurl 'http://swift-proxy:8888/v1/AUTH_%(tenant_id)s'
--adminurl 'http://swift-proxy:8888/v1'
--internalurl 'http://swift-proxy:8888/v1/AUTH_%(tenant_id)s'
```

The following screenshot shows the output of executing the preceding endpoint-create commands:

```
root@swift-proxy:/home/vedams# keystone endpoint-create --service-id a9c2d44442464975bb50e296fcc584b4 --region regionOne --pu
blicurl 'http://swift-proxy:5000/v2.0' --adminurl 'http://swift-proxy:35357/v2.0' --internalurl 'http://swift-proxy:5000/v2.0
'
+-------------+----------------------------------+
| Property    |              Value               |
+-------------+----------------------------------+
|  adminurl   |   http://swift-proxy:35357/v2.0  |
|     id      | cdade3f814ac48c1b1a365839685c18f |
| internalurl |   http://swift-proxy:5000/v2.0   |
|  publicurl  |   http://swift-proxy:5000/v2.0   |
|   region    |            regionOne             |
| service_id  | a9c2d44442464975bb50e296fcc584b4 |
+-------------+----------------------------------+
root@swift-proxy:/home/vedams# keystone endpoint-create --service-id a0ab378728b148fd9c9a0534d1d6a227 --region regionOne --pu
blicurl 'http://swift-proxy:8888/v1/AUTH_%(tenant_id)s' --adminurl 'http://swift-proxy:8888/v1' --internalurl 'http://swift-p
roxy:8888/v1/AUTH_%(tenant_id)s'
+-------------+-----------------------------------------+
| Property    |                  Value                  |
+-------------+-----------------------------------------+
|  adminurl   |          http://swift-proxy:8888/v1     |
|     id      |     479d9efffcd3452a8d90a4c00c35dc04     |
| internalurl | http://swift-proxy:8888/v1/AUTH_%(tenant_id)s |
|  publicurl  | http://swift-proxy:8888/v1/AUTH_%(tenant_id)s |
|   region    |                regionOne                |
| service_id  |     a0ab378728b148fd9c9a0534d1d6a227     |
+-------------+-----------------------------------------+
root@swift-proxy:/home/vedams#
```

11. We will now unset the environment variables that we exported earlier, since we don't need them again. We will be calling the REST APIs, and providing the username and password to them along with the endpoint. Unset the environment variables as shown in the following commands:

```
# unset OS_SERVICE_TOKEN
# unset OS_SERVICE_ENDPOINT
```

12. We will now request an authentication token using the admin user and password. This verifies that the Keystone service is configured and running correctly on the configured endpoint.

    We also verify that authentication is working correctly by requesting the token on a particular tenant as shown in the following command:

```
# keystone --os-username=admin --os-password=ADMIN_PASS \
--os-tenant-name=admin --os-auth-url=http://swift-proxy:35357/v2.0 token-get
```

13. Finally, test the Keystone service by running the following commands below to list out the users, tenants, roles, and endpoints (the previously generated random token is named Random Token):

```
# keystone --os-token=Random Token --os-endpoint=http://swift-proxy:35357/v2.0 \
user-list
# keystone --os-token=Random Token --os-endpoint=http://swift-proxy:35357/v2.0 \
tenant-list
# keystone --os-token=Random Token --os-endpoint=http://swift-proxy:35357/v2.0 \
role-list
# keystone --os-token=Random Token --os-endpoint=http://swift-proxy:35357/v2.0 \
endpoint-list
```

Summary

In this chapter, you learned how to install and set up the OpenStack Swift service to provide object storage, and install and set up the Keystone service to provide authentication for users to access Swift object store. The next chapter provides details on various tools, commands, and APIs that are available to access and use the Swift Object Store.

4
Using Swift

This chapter explains the various mechanisms that are available to access Swift. Using these mechanisms, we will be able to authenticate accounts, list containers, create containers, create objects, delete objects, and so on. Tools and libraries such as Swift Client CLI, cURL client, HTTP REST API, JAVA libraries, Ruby OpenStack libraries, and Python libraries use Swift APIs internally to provide access to the Swift cluster. In particular, we will be using the Swift Client CLI, cURL, and HTTP REST API to access Swift and perform various operations on containers and objects. Also, we will be using EVault's Long-Term Storage (LTS2) cloud storage to demonstrate the use of Swift.

Installing the clients

This section talks about installing cURL and Swift's client CLI command line tools. In this section we describe how to install these tools on a Ubuntu 12.04 Linux operating system. Please refer to the other Linux distribution command sets for installing the clients in those operating systems. Windows and Mac version of these tools are also available. The following commands are used to install the cURL and the Swift Client CLI:

- **cURL**: This is a command-line tool that can be used to transfer data using various protocols. The following command is used to install cURL:

  ```
  # apt-get install curl
  ```

- **Swift Client CLI**: This is a tool to access and perform operations on a Swift cluster. This tool is installed using the following command:

  ```
  # apt-get install python-swiftclient
  ```

- **REST API Client**: To access Swift services via the REST API, we can use third-party tools such as Fiddler web debugger that supports REST's architecture.

Creating a token using authentication

The first step in order to access containers or objects is to authenticate the user by sending a request to the authentication service and get a valid token that can then be used in subsequent commands to perform various operations. We are using Keystone authentication in our configuration and the examples shown in this chapter. There is another method of authentication called Swauth that can be used. It works in a slightly different way, but we don't deal with the details of Swauth here. The following command is used to get the valid keystone authentication token:

```
# curl -X POST -i https://auth.lts2.evault.com/v2.0/Tokens -H 'Content-
type: application/json' -d '{"auth":{"passwordCredentials":{"username":"u
ser","password":"password"},"tenantName":"tenant1"}}'
```

In the preceding command, `https://auth.lts2.evault.com/v2.0` is EVault's authentication endpoint. Along with this the username, password, and the tenant name are also provided.

The token that is generated is shown as follows (it has been truncated for better readability):

```
token = MIIGIwYJKoZIhvcNAQcCoIIGFDCCBhACAQExCTAHBgUrDgMCGjCCBHkGCSqGSI
b3DQEHAaCCBGoEggRme...yJhY2Nlc3MiOiB7InRva2VuIjogeyJpc3N1ZWRfYXQiOiAiMjAx
My0xMS0yNlQwNjoxODo0Mi4zNTA0NTciLCU+KNYN20G7KJOO5bXbbpSAWw+5Vfl8zl6Jq
AKKWENTrlKBvsFzO-peLBwcKZXTpfJkJxqK7Vpzc-NIygSwPWjODs--0WTes+CyoRD
```

This token is then used as a parameter in the commands accessing Swift, for example, in the following command:

```
curl -X HEAD  -i https://storage.lts2.evault.com/v1/26cef4782cca4e5aabbb9
497b8c1ee1b
```

```
-H 'X-Auth-Token: token' -H 'Content-type: application/json'
```

More details on the commands are provided in the upcoming sections.

Displaying metadata information for an account, container, or object

This section describes how we can obtain information about the account, container, or object.

Using the Swift Client CLI

The Swift Client CLI `stat` command is used to get information about the account, container, or object. The name of the container should be provided after the `stat` command to get container information. The name of the container and object should be provided after the `stat` command to get object information.

Execute the following request to display the account status:

```
# swift --os-auth-token=token --os-storage-url= https://storage.lts2.
evault.com/v1/26cef4782cca4e5aabbb9497b8c1ee1b stat
```

In the preceding commands, `token` is the generated token as described in the previous section and `26cef4782cca4e5aabbb9497b8c1ee1b` is the account name.

The response shows the information about the account, which is as follows:

```
Account: 26cef4782cca4e5aabbb9497b8c1ee1b

Containers: 2

Objects: 6

Bytes: 17

Accept-Ranges: bytes

Server: nginx/1.4.1
```

Using cURL

The following command shows how to obtain the same account information using cURL. It shows that the account contains two containers and six objects.

Execute the following request:

```
# curl -X HEAD  -i https://storage.lts2.evault.com/v1/26cef4782cca4e5aabb
b9497b8c1ee1b

-H 'X-Auth-Token: token' -H 'Content-type: application/json'
```

The response to the preceding command is as follows:

```
HTTP/1.1 204 No Content

Server: nginx/1.4.1

Date: Wed, 04 Dec 2013 06:53:13 GMT

Content-Type: text/html; charset=UTF-8

Content-Length: 0
```

```
X-Account-Bytes-Used: 3439364822

X-Account-Container-Count: 2

X-Account-Object-Count: 6
```

Using the REST API

Fiddler web debugger, which supports REST, was used to send the request and receive the HTTP response. Execute the following request:

```
Method : HEAD

URL    : https://storage.lts2.evault.com/v1/26cef4782cca4e5aabbb9497b8c1e
e1b Header :  X-Auth-Token: token

Data   :  No data

The response is as follows:HTTP/1.1 204 No Content

Server: nginx/1.4.1

Date: Wed, 04 Dec 2013 06:47:17 GMT

Content-Type: text/html; charset=UTF-8

Content-Length: 0

X-Account-Bytes-Used: 3439364822

X-Account-Container-Count: 2

X-Account-Object-Count: 6
```

As you can see, this is a different mechanism of issuing the command, but is very similar to accessing the Swift cluster using cURL.

Listing containers

This section describes how to obtain information about the containers present in an account.

Using the Swift Client CLI

Execute the following request:

```
swift --os-auth-token=token --os-storage-url= https://storage.lts2.
evault.com/v1/26cef4782cca4e5aabbb9497b8c1ee1b list
```

The response to the preceding request is as follows:

```
cities

countries
```

Using cURL

The following command shows how to obtain the same containers information using cURL. It shows that the account comprises of two containers and six objects.

Execute the following request:

```
curl -X GET -i https://storage.lts2.evault.com/v1/26cef4782cca4e5aabbb949
7b8c1ee1b -H 'X-Auth_token: token'
```

The response to the request is as follows:

```
HTTP/1.1 200 OK
X-Account-Container-Count: 2
X-Account-Object-Count: 6


cities
countries
```

Here we see that the output has header and body, whereas in the previous example, we only had header and no body in the output.

Listing objects in a container

This section describes how to list the objects that are present in a container.

Using the Swift Client CLI

The following command shows how to list objects using the Swift Client CLI (in this example we are listing out the objects in the cities container):

Execute the following request:

```
swift --os-auth-token=token --os-storage-url= https://storage.lts2.
evault.com/v1/26cef4782cca4e5aabbb9497b8c1ee1b list cities
```

The response to the request is as follows:

```
London.txt
Mumbai.txt
NewYork.txt
```

Using cURL

The following command shows how to list objects using cURL. In this example, we list the objects in the Cities container.

Execute the following request:

```
curl -X GET -i https://storage.lts2.evault.com/v1/26cef4782cca4e5aabbb949
7b8c1ee1b/cities

-H 'X-Auth-Token: token '
```

The response of the request is as follows:

```
HTTP/1.1 200 OK

Content-Type: text/plain; charset=utf-8

Content-Length: 34

X-Container-Object-Count: 3


London.txt

Mumbai.txt

NewYork.txt
```

Using the REST API

In this example, we list the objects in the countries container.

Execute the following request:

```
Method : GET

URL    : URL    : https://storage.lts2.evault.com/v1/26cef4782cca4e5aabbb
9497b8c1ee1b/countries

Header :   X-Auth-Token: token

Data   : No content
```

The response to the request is as follows:

```
HTTP/1.1 200 OK

Content-Type: text/plain; charset=utf-8

Content-Length: 38

X-Container-Object-Count: 3


France.txt

India.txt

UnitedStates.txt
```

Updating the metadata for a container

This section describes how to add or update metadata for a container.

Using the Swift Client CLI

In this example, we are adding metadata for countries that we have visited.

Execute the following request:

```
swift --os-auth-token=token --os-storage-url= https://storage.lts2.
evault.com/v1/26cef4782cca4e5aabbb9497b8c1ee1b post countries

-H "X-Container-Meta-Countries: visited"
```

Using the REST API

Here we are adding metadata using the REST API.

Execute the following request:

```
Method : POST
URL    : https://storage.lts2.evault.com/v1/26cef4782cca4e5aabbb9497b8c1e
e1b/countries
Header :  X-Auth-Token: token
         X-Container-Meta-Countries: visited
Data   : No content
```

Environment variables

The following environment variables can be used to simplify the CLI commands:

- OS_USERNAME: This contains the username to access the account
- OS_PASSWORD: This contains the password associated with the username
- OS_TENANT_NAME: This contains the name of the tenant
- OS_AUTH_URL: This contains the authentication URL

Once these environment variables are exported, we no longer have to pass these values as input parameters when running the Swift CLI tools.

Pseudo-hierarchical directories

OpenStack Swift object storage can simulate a hierarchical directory structure in containers by including a / (forward slash character) in the object's name.

Let's upload a file (AMERICA/USA/Newyork.txt) into the Continent container using the following command:

```
# swift upload Continent AMERICA/USA/Newyork.txt
```

Let's list the Continent container that has a few pseudo-hierarchical folders by using the following commands:

```
# swift list Continent
AMERICA/USA/Newyork.txt
ASIA/ASIA.txt
ASIA/China/China.txt
ASIA/INDIA/India.txt
Australia/Australia.txt
continent.txt
```

We can use / as the delimiter parameter to limit the displayed results. We can also use the prefix parameter along with the delimiter parameter to view the objects in the pseudo directory along with pseudo directories within that. The following are a couple of examples showing the use of these parameters:

```
# swift list Continent --delimiter /
AMERICA/
ASIA/
Australia/
continent.txt

# swift list Continent --delimiter / --prefix ASIA/
ASIA/ASIA.txt
ASIA/China/
ASIA/INDIA/

# swift list Continent --delimiter / --prefix ASIA/INDIA/
ASIA/INDIA/India.txt
```

Container ACLs

As we saw in the previous sections, in order to access containers and objects, a valid **auth** token has to be sent in the X-Auth-Token header with each request. Otherwise, an authorization failure code will be returned. In certain cases, access needs to be provided to other clients and applications for certain containers and objects. Access can be provided by setting a metadata element for the container called X-Container-Read. The following example sets this **Access Control Lists (ACL)** to the cities container:

First, let us list the container status that shows the lack of ACL. Run the following command with admin privileges (the admin user will have the permissions to run this command):

```
swift stat cities
```

The values for Read ACL and Write ACL in the following response indicates the lack of ACL:

```
Account: 26cef4782cca4e5aabbb9497b8c1ee1b
Container: cities
Objects: 3
Read ACL:
Write ACL:
Sync To:
```

When the tenant1:user1 user, who does not have access to this container, tries to access this container, a forbidden error message is returned.

Execute the following request:

```
swift -V 2.0 -A https://auth.lts2.evault.com/v2.0 -U tenant1:user1 -K t1
list cities
```

A forbidden error message is returned as the response. This error is as follows:

```
Container GET failed: 403 Forbidden
Access was denied to this resource
```

In the preceding example, the username is provided using the -U option and the key to access the account is provided using the -K option.

Now, let's set the X-Container-Read metadata element and enable READ access for tenant1:user1. This operation can only be done by the admin user by using the following command:

```
swift post -r tenant1:user1 cities
```

To check the ACL permissions, we execute the following command:

```
swift stat cities
```

The response to the preceding command is as follows:

```
Account: 26cef4782cca4e5aabbb9497b8c1ee1b
Container: cities
Objects: 3
Read ACL: tenant1:user1
Write ACL:
Sync To:
```

Now, when the `tenant1:user1` user tries to access this container, access is granted and the command is successfully executed.

Execute the following request:

```
swift -V 2.0 -A https://auth.lts2.evault.com/v2.0 -U tenant1:user1 -K t1 list cities
```

The response to the request is as follows:

```
London.txt
Mumbai.txt
NewYork.txt
```

Since the `X-Container-Write` ACL is not set for the `tenant1:user1` user for the `cities` container, this user cannot write to the `cities` container. In order to allow write access, let's set the `X-Container-Write` ACL as follows:

```
swift post -w tenant1:user1 cities
```

To check the ACL permissions, we execute the following command:

```
swift stat cities
```

The response to the preceding command is as follows:

```
Account: 26cef4782cca4e5aabbb9497b8c1ee1b
Container: cities
Objects: 3
Read ACL: tenant1:user1
Write ACL: tenant1:user1
Sync To:
```

Now the `tenant1:user1` user will be able to write objects into the `cities` container.

If we want to give access to a large number of users, ACLs such as .r:*, .rlistings can be used. The .r:* prefix allows any user to retrieve objects from the container and .rlistings turns on listing for the container.

Transferring large objects

As discussed in *Chapter 2*, *OpenStack Swift Architecture*, Swift limits a single object upload to 5 GB. Larger objects can be split into 5 GB or smaller segments by specifying the segment-size option in the swift CLI tool command-line argument and uploaded to a special container (created within the container where the object is being uploaded to).

Once the upload has been completed, a manifest object has to be created that contains information about the segments. The manifest file is of zero size with headers such as X-Object-Manifest identifying the special container in which the segments are stored and the name with which all the segments will start. For example, if we have to upload France.txt, which is of size 8 GB, to the countries container, then the France.txt object has to be split into two chunks (5 GB and 3 GB). The chunk object's name will start with France.txt (France. txt/../00000000 and France.txt/../00000001).

A special container called countries_segments will be created and the chunks will be uploaded to this container. A manifest object called France.txt will be created in the countries container. The manifest file will have zero size and will contain the following header. (It is not mandatory to have the segments placed in a special container and they can as well exist in the same container):

```
X-Object-Manifest: countries_segments/France.txt
```

When a download request is made for the large-sized object, Swift will automatically concatenate all the segments and download the entire large-sized object.

The Swift Client CLI has the -S flag, to specify the segment size, which can be used to split a large object into segments and upload. The following command is used to upload a file with a segment size of 5368709120 bytes:

```
Make the following request:
```

```
swift upload countries -S 5368709120 France.txt
```

The response to the preceding commands is as follows:

```
France.txt segment 0
France.txt segment 1
France.txt segment 2
France.txt
```

The following command can be used to list out the containers present:

```
Swift list
```

The response to the preceding command is as follows:

```
Countries
Countries_segments
cities
```

The following command lists the objects in the countries_segments container:

```
Swift list countries_segments
```

The response to the preceding command is as follows:

```
France.txt/1385989364.105938/5368709120/00000000
France.txt/1385989364.105938/5368709120/00000001
```

Amazon S3 API compatibility

Users familiar with the Amazon S3 API and accessing S3 buckets and objects can access Swift using S3 compatible APIs with the help of Swift3 middleware.

Here, we will show the steps required for one method that uses S3 APIs to access Swift's object store. These steps explain how to install the necessary tools and packages, create credentials, and update the configuration files.

The following steps are performed on the proxy-server node that is running the Ubuntu 12.04 Linux distribution:

1. First, the user requires EC2 credentials (access key and secret key). The keystone user-list and keystone tenant-list commands can be used to obtain the user ID and tenant ID of the user. The following command can be used to create these keys (these need to be run from the proxy server):

   ```
   keystone ec2-credentials-create --user-
   id 916673a90b8749e18f0ee3ec5bf17ab9 --tenant-id
   6530edfe037242d1ac8bb07b7fd76046
   ```

   The response is as follows:

   ```
   +----------+----------------------------------+
   | Property |              Value               |
   +----------+----------------------------------+
   |  access  | 1178d235dbd84d48b417170ec9aed72c |
   |  secret  | c4ea0a8fbf7d4a469f6d0fb5cdb47d5b |
   ```

```
|  tenant_id  |  6530edfe037242d1ac8bb07b7fd76046  |
|   user_id   |  916673a90b8749e18f0ee3ec5bf17ab9  |
```

2. Install the Swift3 package by running the following commands (these commands require Git to be installed on your system):

```
# sudo git clone https://github.com/fujita/swift3.git
# cd swift3
# sudo python setup.py install
```

3. Install the libdigest-hmac-perl package by running the following command (this package is used for integrity checking between two entities that share a secret key):

```
apt-get install libdigest-hmac-perl
```

4. Edit the proxy-server.conf file and make the following changes if you want to use the keystone authentication:

   ° Change the pipeline line in the proxy server.conf file to:

```
[pipeline:main]
pipeline = catch_errors cache swift3 s3token authtoken
keystone proxy-server
```

   ° Add a Swift3 WSGI filter to the proxy-server.conf file using the following command:

```
[filter:swift3]
use = egg:swift3#swift3
```

   ° Add the s3token filter as in the following commands:

```
[filter:s3token]
paste.filter_factory = keystone.middleware.s3_token:filter_
factory
auth_port = 35357
auth_host = 127.0.0.1
auth_protocol = http
```

   ° Restart the proxy service using the following command:

```
Service swift-proxy restart
```

5. The following steps should be performed on the client that will access Swift Object Store:

   ° Since we will use s3curl to execute the S3 commands, download s3-curl.zip from the following link:

```
http://s3.amazonaws.com/doc/s3-example-code/s3-curl.zip
```

- ° Install the wget utility prior to running the following command:

```
wget http://s3.amazonaws.com/doc/s3-example-code/s3-curl.zip
```

- ° Unzip s3-curl.zip and provide executable access to the s3curl.pl file.

- ° Create a .s3curl file and change the ID and key of personal account with the EC2 credentials (access and secret keys) that were given to the user. We are using vi editor to create the file as shown in the following:

```
#vi  ~/.s3curl
%awsSecretAccessKeys = (
# personal account
  personal => {
    id => '1178d235dbd84d48b417170ec9aed72c',
    key => 'c4ea0a8fbf7d4a469f6d0fb5cdb47d5b',
  },
# corporate account
work => {
    id => '1ATXQ3HHA59CYF1CVS02',
    key => 'WQY4SrSS95pJUT95V6zWea01gBKBCL6PI0cdxeH8',
  },
);
```

Accessing Swift using S3 commands

In this section, we will give examples of S3 commands to perform various operations.

- **List buckets:** This command lists all the buckets for this user. Buckets in S3 are similar to containers in Swift.

```
# ./s3curl.pl --id=personal -- https://auth.lts2.evault.com -v
```

The response is as follows:

```
<?xml version="1.0" encoding="UTF-8"?><ListAllMyBucketsResult
xmlns="http://doc.s3.amazonaws.com/2006-03-01"><Buckets>

  <Bucket><Name>cities</Name><CreationDate>2009-02-
03T16:45:09.000Z</CreationDate></Bucket>

  <Bucket><Name>countries</Name><CreationDate>2009-02-
03T16:45:09.000Z</CreationDate></Bucket>

  </Buckets></ListAllMyBucketsResult>
```

- **List objects in a bucket**: This command lists all the objects present in the specified bucket. Let us list all the objects in the `cities` bucket by using the following command:

```
# ./s3curl.pl --id=personal -- https://auth.lts2.evault.com/cities
-v
```

- **Create a Bucket**: The following command creates a bucket called `continents`:

```
# ./s3curl.pl --id=personal --createBucket -- -v https://auth.
lts2.evault.com/continents
```

- **Delete a Bucket**: The following command deletes a bucket called `continents`:

```
# ./s3curl.pl --id=personal --delete -- -v https://auth.lts2.
evault.com/continents
```

Accessing Swift using client libraries

There are several libraries available in Java, Python, Ruby, PHP, and other programming languages to access the Swift cluster. Applications can be simplified using these libraries. Let us explore a few libraries.

Java

The Apache jclouds library (`http://jclouds.apache.org/documentation/quickstart/rackspace/`), particularly the `org.jclouds.openstack.swift.CommonSwiftClient` API can be used to write applications in Java to connect to Swift and perform various operations on accounts, containers, and objects.

A sample code is shown as follows:

```
import org.jclouds.ContextBuilder;
import org.jclouds.blobstore.BlobStore;
import org.jclouds.blobstore.BlobStoreContext;
import org.jclouds.openstack.swift.CommonSwiftAsyncClient;
import org.jclouds.openstack.swift.CommonSwiftClient;

BlobStoreContext context = ContextBuilder.newBuilder(provider)
          .endpoint("http://auth.lts2.evault.com/")
          .credentials(user, password)
          .modules(modules)
          .buildView(BlobStoreContext.class);
storage = context.getBlobStore();
```

```
swift = context.unwrap();
containers = swift.getApi().listContainers();
objects = swift.getApi().listObjects(myContainer);
```

Python

The python-swiftclient library provides Python language bindings for OpenStack Swift. After authentication, the following sample code shows how to list containers:

```
#!/usr/bin/env python

http_connection = http_connection(url)
cont = get_container(url, token, container, marker, limit, prefix,
delimiter, end_marker, path, http_conn)
```

More information about the library is provided at `https://github.com/openstack/python-swiftclient/`.

Ruby

The ruby-openstack library (`https://github.com/ruby-openstack/ruby-openstack`) provides ruby bindings for the OpenStack cloud. The following sample code shows how to list containers and objects:

```
Lts2 = OpenStack::Connection.create(:username => USER, :api_key =>
API_KEY, :authtenant => TENANT, :auth_url => API_URL, :service_type =>
"object-store")
Lts2.containers
=>["cities" , "countries"]

Cont = Lts2.container("cities")
Cont.objects
=>[" London.txt"," Mumbai.txt"," NewYork.txt"]
```

Summary

In this chapter, you learned how to use various Swift clients to interact with Swift clusters and get information on accounts, containers, and objects. You were introduced to ACLs, large object transfers, and also to various Swift client libraries that can be used to write applications in your desired language such as Java, Ruby, and Python.

The next chapter talks about managing Swift and things to consider while replacing or expanding disks, nodes, and zones. It also provides information on various tools that can be used to gather information on the object storage behavior.

5
Managing Swift

After a Swift cluster has been installed and deployed, it needs to be managed to serve customer expectations and service level agreements. Since there are several components in a Swift cluster, it is a little different, and hence more difficult to manage compared to traditional storage. There are several tools and mechanisms an administrator can use to effectively manage a Swift cluster. This chapter deals with these aspects in more detail.

Routine management

The Swift cluster consists of several proxy server nodes and storage server nodes. These nodes run many processes and services to keep the cluster up and running, and provide overall availability. Any kind of general server management tools/applications such as Nagios, which is described later in the chapter, can be run to track the state of the general services, CPU utilization, memory utilization, disk subsystem performance, and so on. Looking at the system logs is a great way to detect impending failures. Along with this, there are some tools to monitor the Swift services in particular. Some of them are Swift Recon, Swift StatsD, Swift Dispersion, and Swift Informant.

Nagios is a monitoring framework that comprises several plugins that can be used to monitor network services (such as HTTP and SSH), processor load, performance, and CPU and disk utilization. It also provides remote monitoring capabilities by running scripts remotely connected to the monitored system using SSH or SSL. Users can write their own plugins depending on their requirements to extend these monitoring capabilities. These plugins can be written in several languages such as Perl, Ruby, C++, and Python. Nagios also provides a notification mechanism where an administrator can be alerted when problems occur on the system. The following figure shows how to integrate a monitoring solution based on Nagios:

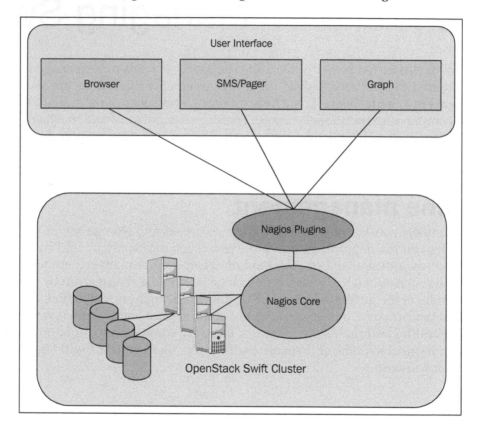

More information on Nagios can be found at www.nagios.org. Next, let us look into the details of Swift monitoring tools.

Swift cluster monitoring

In this section, we describe various tools that are available to monitor the Swift clusters. We also show snapshots from the Vedams Swift monitoring application that integrates data from various Swift monitoring tools.

Swift Recon

Swift Recon is a middleware software that is configured on the object server node and sits in the data path. A local cache directory, which is used to store logs, needs to be specified during setup. It comes with the swift-recon command-line tool which can be used to access and display the various metrics that are being tracked. You can use `swift-recon -h` to get help with using the swift-recon tool.

Some of the general server metrics that are tracked are as follows:

- Load averages
- The `/proc/meminfo` data
- Mounted filesystems
- Unmounted drives
- Socket statistics

Along with these, some of the following Swift stats are also tracked:

- MD5checksums of account, container, and object ring
- Replication information
- Number of quarantined accounts, containers, and objects

The following screenshot shows Swift Recon data within the Vedams Swift monitoring application:

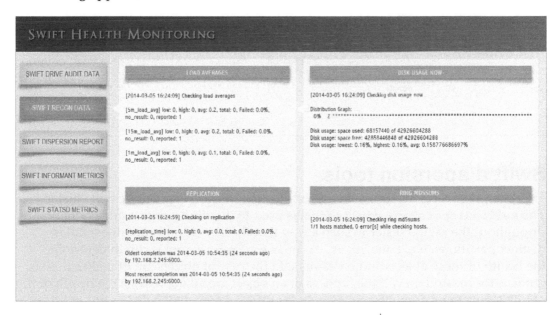

Swift Informant

Swift Informant is also a middleware software that gives insight to client requests to the proxy server. This software sits in the proxy server's data path and provides the following metrics to the StatsD server:

- Status code for requests to account, container, or object
- Duration of the request and time until `start_response` metric was seen
- Bytes transferred in the request

Swift Informant can be downloaded from `https://github.com/pandemicsyn/swift-informant`.

The following screenshot displays the Swift Informant data within the Vedams Swift monitoring application:

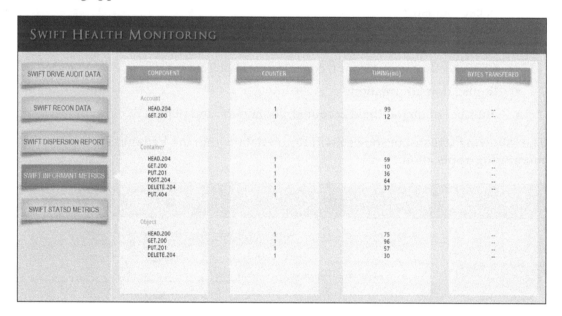

Swift dispersion tools

This postprocessing tool is used to determine the overall health of a Swift cluster. The `swift-dispersion-populate` tool is used to distribute objects and containers throughout the Swift cluster in such a way that the objects and containers fall in distinct partitions. Next, the `swift-dispersion-report` tool is run to determine the health of these objects and containers. In the case of objects, Swift makes three replicas for redundancy. If the replicas of an object are all good, then the health of the object is said to be good; the `swift-dispersion-report` tool helps figure out this health of all objects and containers within the cluster.

The following screenshot displays the Swift Dispersion data within the Vedams Swift monitoring application:

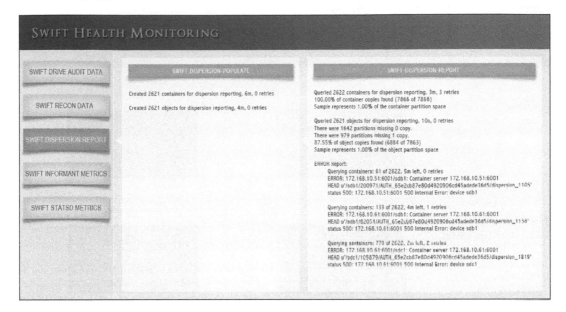

StatsD

Swift services have been instrumented to send statistics (counters and logs) directly to a StatsD server that is configured.

A simple StatsD daemon to receive the metrics can be found at https://github.com/etsy/statsd/.

The StatsD metrics are provided in real time and can help identify problems as they occur. Configuration files containing the following parameters should be set in the Swift configuration files to enable StatsD logging:

- `log_statsd_host`
- `log_statsd_port`
- `log_statsd_default_sample_rate`
- `log_statsd_sample_rate_factor`
- `log_statsd_metric_prefix`

The `statsd_sample_rate_factor` parameter can be adjusted to set the logging frequency. The `log_statsd_metric_prefix` parameter is configured on a node to prepend this prefix to every metric sent to the StatsD server from this node. If the `log_statsd_host` entry is not set, then this functionality will be disabled.

The StatsD logs can be sent to a backend Graphite server to display the metrics as graphs. The following screenshot of the Vedams Swift monitoring application represents the StatsD logs as graphs:

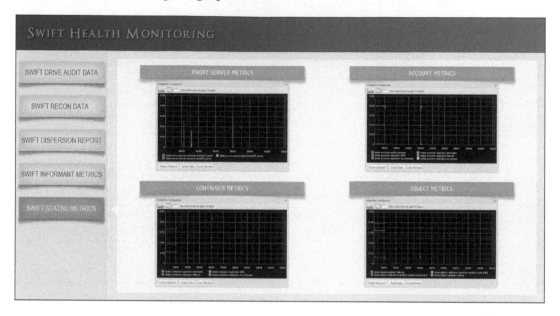

Swift metrics

The Swift source code has metrics logging (counters, timings, and so on) built into it. Some of the metrics sent to the StatsD server from various Swift services are listed in the table. They have been classified based on the **Create, Read, Update, Delete (CRUD)** operations:

Create/PUT	Read/GET	Update/POST	Delete
account-server. PUT.errors. timing	account-server. GET.errors. timing	account-server. POST.errors. timing	account-server. DELETE.errors. timing
account-server. PUT.timing	account-server. GET.timing	account-server. POST.timing	account-server. DELETE.timing
container-server.PUT. errors.timing	container-server.GET. errors.timing	container-server.POST. errors.timing	container-server.DELETE. errors.timing
container-server.PUT. timing	container-server.GET. timing	container-server.POST. timing	container-server.DELETE. timing

Create/PUT	Read/GET	Update/POST	Delete
object-server. async_pendings	object-server. GET.errors. timing	object-server. POST.errors. timing	object-server. async_pendings
object-server. PUT.errors. timing	object-server. GET.timing	object-server. POST.timing	object-server. DELETE.errors. timing
object-server. PUT.timeouts	proxy- server.<type>. client_timeouts	proxy- server.<type>. <verb>.<status>. timing	object-server. DELETE.timing
object-server. PUT.timing	proxy- server.<type>. <verb>.<status>. timing	proxy- server.<type>. <verb>.<status>. xfer	proxy- server.<type>. <verb>.<status>. timing
object-server. PUT.<device>. timing	proxy- server.<type>. <verb>.<status>. xfer		proxy- server.<type>. <verb>.<status>. xfer
proxy- server.<type>. client_timeouts			
proxy- server.<type>. client_ disconnects			
proxy- server.<type>. <verb>.<status>. timing			
proxy- server.<type>. <verb>. <status>.xfer			

Logging using rsyslog

It is very useful to get logs from various Swift services and that can be achieved by configuring proxy-server.conf and rsyslog. In order to receive logs from the proxy server, we modify the /etc/swift/proxy-server.conf configuration file by adding the following lines:

```
log_name = name
log_facility = LOG_LOCALx
log_level = LEVEL
```

Let's describe the preceding entries: name can be any name that you would like to see in the logs. The letter x in LOG_LOCALx can be any number between zero and seven. The LEVEL parameter can be either emergency, alert, critical, error, warning, notification, informational, or debug.

Next, we modify /etc/rsyslog.conf to add the following line of code in the GLOBAL_DIRECTIVES section:

```
$PrivDropToGroup adm
```

Also, we create a config file /etc/rsyslog.d/swift.conf and add the following line of code to it:

```
local2.*          /var/log/swift/proxy.log
```

The preceding line tells syslog that any log written to the LOG_LOCAL2 facility should go to the /var/log/swift/proxy.log file. We then give permissions for access to the /var/log/swift folder, and restart the proxy service and syslog service.

Failure management

In this section, we deal with detecting failures and actions to rectify failures. There can be drive, server, zone, or even region failures. As described in *Chapter 2, OpenStack Swift Architecture,* Swift is designed for availability and tolerance to partial failure (where entire parts of the cluster can fail) during the CAP theorem discussion.

Detecting drive failure

Kernel logs are a good place to look for drive failures. The disk subsystem will log warnings or errors that can help an administrator determine whether drives are going bad or have already failed. We can also set up a script on storage nodes to capture drive failure information using the drive audit process described in *Chapter 2, OpenStack Swift Architecture,* executing the following steps:

1. On each storage node, create a script swift-drive-audit in the /etc/swift folder with the following contents:

```
[drive-audit]
log_facility = LOG_LOCAL0
log_level = DEBUG
device_dir = /srv/node
minutes = 60
error_limit = 2
log_file_pattern = /var/log/kern*
regex_pattern_X = berrorb.*b(sd[a-z]{1,2}d?)b and b(sd[a-z]{1,2}
d?)b.*berrorb
```

2. Add the following line of code to `/etc/rsyslog.d/swift.conf`:

   `local0.*    /var/log/swift/drive-audit`

3. We then restart the rsyslog service using the following command:

   `Service rsyslog restart`

4. We then restart the Swift services using the following command:

   `swift-init rest restart`

5. The drive failure information will now be stored in the `/var/log/swift/drive-audit` log file.

Handling drive failure

When a drive failure occurs, we can either replace the drive quickly at a later time or not replace it at all. If we do not plan to replace the drive immediately, then it is better to unmount the drive and remove it from the ring. If we decide to replace the drive, then we take out the failed drive and replace it with a good drive, format it, and mount it. We will let the replication algorithm take care of filling this drive with data to maintain consistent replicas and data integrity.

Handling node failure

When a storage server in a Swift cluster is experiencing problems, we have to determine whether the problem can be fixed in a short interval, such as a couple of hours, or if it will take an extended period of time. If the downtime interval is small, we can let Swift services work around the failure while we debug and fix the issue with the node. Since Swift maintains multiple replicas of data (the default is three), there won't be a problem of data availability, but the timings for data access might increase. As soon as the problem is found and fixed and the node is brought back up, Swift replication services will take care of figuring out the missing information and will update the nodes and get them in sync.

If the node repair time is extended, then it is better to remove the node and all associated devices from the ring. Once the node is brought back online, the devices can be formatted, remounted, and added back to the ring.

The two following commands are useful to remove devices and nodes from the ring:

- To remove a device from the ring, use:

  `swift-ring-builder <builder-file> remove <ip_address>/<device_name>`

  For example, `swift-ring-builder account.builder remove 172.168.10.52/sdb1`.

- To remove a server from the ring, use:

  ```
  swift-ring-builder <builder-file> remove <ip_address>
  ```

  For example, `swift-ring-builder account.builder remove 172.168.10.52`.

Proxy server failure

If there is only one proxy server in the cluster and it goes down, then there is a chance that no objects can be accessed (upload or download) by the client, so this needs immediate attention. This is why it is always a good idea to have a redundant proxy server to increase data availability in the Swift cluster. After identifying and fixing the failure in the proxy server, the Swift services are restarted and object store access is restored.

Zone and region failure

When a complete zone fails, it is still possible that the Swift services are not interrupted because of the High Availability configuration that contains multiple storage nodes and multiple zones. The storage servers and drives belonging to the failed node have to be brought back into service if the failure can be debugged quickly. Otherwise, the storage servers and drives that belong to the zone have to be removed from the ring, and the ring needs to be rebalanced. Once the zone is brought back into service, the drives and storage servers can be added back into the ring and the ring can be rebalanced. In general, a zone failure should be dealt with as a critical issue. In some cases, the top-of-the-rack storage or network switch can have failures, thus disconnecting storage arrays and servers from the Swift cluster, leading to zone failures. In these cases, the switch failures have to be diagnosed and rectified quickly.

In a multiregion setup, if there is a region failure, then all requests can be routed to the surviving regions. The servers and drives that belong to the region need to be brought back into service quickly to balance the load that is currently being handled by the surviving regions. In other words, this failure should be dealt as a blocker issue. There can be latencies observed in uploads and downloads due to the requests being routed to different regions. Region failures can also occur due to failures occurring in core routers or firewalls. These failures should also be quickly diagnosed and rectified to bring the region back into service.

Capacity planning

As more clients start accessing the Swift cluster, it will increase demand for additional storage. With Swift, this is easy to accomplish; you can simply add more storage nodes and associated proxy servers. This section deals with the planning and adding of new storage drives as well as storage servers.

Adding new drives

Though adding new drives is a straightforward process, it requires careful planning since this involves rebalancing of the ring. Once we decide to add new drives, we will add these drives to a particular storage server in a zone by formatting and mounting these drives. Next, we will run the swift-ring-builder `add` commands to add the drives to the ring. Finally, we will run the `swift-ring-builder rebalance` command to rebalance the ring. The generated `.gz` ring files need to be distributed to all the storage server nodes. The commands to perform these operations were explained in *Chapter 3, Installing OpenStack Swift*, in the *Formatting and mounting hard disks* and *Ring setup* sections.

Often, we end up replacing old drives with bigger and better drives. In this scenario, rather than executing an abrupt move, it is better to slowly start migrating data off the old drive to other drives by reducing the weight of the drive in the ring and repeating this step a few times. Once data has been moved off this drive, it can be safely removed. After removing the old drive, simply insert the new drive and follow the previously mentioned steps to add this drive to the ring.

Adding new storage and proxy servers

Adding new storage and proxy servers is also a straightforward process, where new servers need to be provisioned according to the instructions provided in *Chapter 3, Installing OpenStack Swift*. Storage servers need to be placed in the right zones, and drives that belong to these servers need to be added to the ring. After rebalancing and distributing the `.gz` ring files to the rest of the storage servers, the new storage servers are now part of the cluster. Similarly, after setting up a new proxy server, the configuration files and load balancing settings need to be updated. This proxy server is now part of the cluster and can start accepting requests from users.

Migrations

This section deals with hardware and software migrations. The migrations can be to either existing servers or to new servers within a zone or region. As new hardware and software (operating system, packages, or Swift software) becomes available, the existing servers and software need to be migrated to take advantage of faster processor speeds and latest software updates. It is a good idea to upgrade one server at a time and one zone at a time since Swift services can deal with an entire zone being migrated.

The following steps are required to upgrade a storage server node:

1. Execute the following command to stop all the Swift operations running in the background:

   ```
   swift-init rest stop
   ```

2. Gracefully shutdown all the Swift services by using the following command line:

   ```
   swift-init {account|container|object} shutdown
   ```

3. Upgrade the necessary operating system and system software packages, and install/upgrade the Swift package required. In general, Swift is on a six-month update cycle.

4. Next, create or perform the required changes to the Swift configuration files.

5. After rebooting the server, restart all the required services by executing the following commands:

   ```
   swift-init {account|container|object} start
   swift-init rest start
   ```

If there are changes with respect to the drives on the storage server, we have to make sure we update and rebalance the ring.

Once we have completed migration to the new server, we check the log files for proper operation of the server. If the server is operating without any issues, we then proceed to upgrade the next storage server.

Next, we discuss how to upgrade proxy servers. We can make use of the load balancer to isolate the proxy server that we plan to upgrade so that client requests are not sent to this proxy server.

We perform the following steps to upgrade the proxy server:

1. Gracefully shut down the proxy services by using the following command line:

   ```
   swift-init proxy shutdown
   ```

2. Upgrade the necessary operating system, system software packages, and install/upgrade the Swift package required.

3. Next, create or perform the required changes to the Swift proxy configuration files.

4. After rebooting the server, restart all the required services by using the following command:

   ```
   swift-init proxy start
   ```

We then have to make sure that we add the upgraded proxy server back into the load balancer pool so that it can start receiving client requests.

After the upgrade, we have to make sure that the proxy server is operating correctly by monitoring the log files.

Summary

In this chapter, you learned how to manage a Swift cluster, the various tools available to monitor and manage the Swift cluster, and the various metrics to determine the health of the cluster. You also learned what actions need to be taken if a component fails in the cluster and how a cluster can be extended by adding new disks and nodes.

6
Choosing the Right Hardware

Users who utilize OpenStack Swift as a private cloud will be faced with the task of hardware selection. This chapter walks you through all the hardware you need to select, the criteria to be used, and finally a vendor-selection strategy. If you are using a public cloud, the only hardware you can select is the cloud gateway so you can skip this chapter.

The hardware list

The list of minimal hardware required to implement Swift is as follows:

Item	Description
Storage servers	These are physical servers that run the object server software and generally also run the account and container server software. Storage servers require disks to store objects.
Proxy server(s)	These are physical servers that run the proxy server software. At least one is required.
Network switch(es)	*Chapter 3, Installing OpenStack Swift,* describes the various networks required. At a minimum, one switch is required.

The following is a list of optional hardware that may need to be purchased:

Item	Description
Account servers	For large installations where container listings and updates are overwhelming the storage servers, separate account servers may be needed.
Container servers	For large installations where object listings and updates are overwhelming the storage servers, separate container servers may be needed.

Item	Description
Auth servers	For large installations where user authentication is overwhelming the proxy servers, separate auth servers may be needed.
JBODs	For installations where disk density is important, a storage server may be connected to a **JBOD (just a bunch of disks)** using a SAS connection to increase the disk density.
Load balancer / SSL acceleration	This is useful to provide a single IP address for the entire cluster (there are software mechanisms to accomplish this as well, but these are not covered in this book). The SSL functionality in the load balancer offloads software SSL in the proxy server.
Firewall and security appliances	For public, community, and some private networks, firewall and security appliances such as intrusion detection/prevention may be required depending on your company's security policies.
On-premise cloud gateway	To adapt applications that have not ported to the REST HTTP APIs yet, you will need a protocol translation device that converts a familiar file and blocks protocols to REST APIs. This device is called a cloud gateway and is the only piece of hardware that you may need even with a public cloud.

To complicate things even further, each server has the following numerous design elements to configure:

- **CPU performance**: The CPU performance is specified in terms of the number of processors and number of cores/processors. This has the most direct impact on the server's performance.

- **Memory**: The next important consideration is the amount of DRAM memory, which is specified in GB.

- **Flash memory**: Flash memory is another critical performance consideration and is typically in the TB range.

- **Disk/JBOD**: For storage servers, you need to specify the number of disks and types of disks (interface, speed, rating, and so on). These disks could be in the server, connected via a JBOD, or a combination.

- **Network I/O**: A server needs network I/O connectivity via a **LAN-on-motherboard (LOM)** or an add-on **network interface card (NIC)**. This is typically 1 Gbps or 10 Gbps in terms of speed.

- **Hardware management**: Servers vary widely in hardware management features, starting with rudimentary monitoring only through the operating system, OS independent IPMI, to sophisticated remote KVM and remote storage.

The hardware selection criteria

Clearly, the universe of hardware to choose from and the elements within each server are mind boggling. Furthermore, the ratio of proxy to account to container to storage servers is yet another complication. Before we go through the systematic selection criteria, you need to determine the following characteristics about your environment:

- **Point of optimization for your environment**: You will need to decide whether you care more about performance or cost.

- **Scale**: Scale also has a huge impact on hardware selection. For simplicity, let's say *small* is in the hundreds of TB range, *medium* is in the PB range, and *large* is in the tens of PB range and beyond. You will need to determine what range you are in.

The process for choosing hardware is as follows.

Step 1 – choosing the storage server configuration

For small and medium installations, the storage server can include the object, account and container server software. For large installations, we would recommend a separate account and/or container servers. For performance-optimized clusters, the aggregate disk performance must match the total performance of other server components (CPU, memory, flash, and I/O). For cost-optimized clusters, the disk performance can exceed the performance of other components (in other words, saving money to throttle performance). In fact, consider attaching JBODs to really get great disk density.

A higher disk density also results in slight reliability degradation since a node failure takes longer to self-heal, and two additional failures (if you have three copies) have a slightly higher probability of occurring during this longer duration. Of course, the probability of two failures occurring in one self-heal window is very low in both cases. The following figure denotes a storage server with disks (of course, an optional JBOD may also be connected to it):

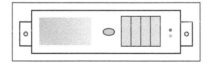

The OpenStack configuration guide (`http://docs.openstack.org/havana/ install-guide/install/apt/content/object-storage-system-requirements. html`) recommends the following server specifications:

- **Processor**: Dual quad-core.
- **Memory**: 8 to 12 GB.
- **Network I/O**: 1 x 1 Gbps NIC. Cost permitting, our recommendation would be to go beyond the official recommendation and use 10 Gbps.

RAID should not be turned on due to performance degradation (there is an exception: if you want to ensure consistency even with a full power loss, you may need to consider RAID).

Finally, a key consideration is the type of disk: enterprise or desktop. Within enterprise disks, there are 15K, 10K, or 7.2K **rotations per minute** (**RPM**) drives and a variety of capacity configurations. For small and medium installations, you might want to consider enterprise drives as they are more reliable than desktop drives. Most small and medium installations are typically not set up to deal with the higher failure rate of desktop drives. The performance and capacity that you choose for an enterprise drive obviously depends on your specific requirements.

For large installations that are *also* very cost-sensitive, you may want to consider desktop drives. The density of desktop drives (up to 6 TB at the time of writing) also contributes favorably to large installations. In addition to the reliability, desktop drives are not specified to be able to run 24 x 7. This means that your IT staff has to be sophisticated enough to deal with a large number of failures and/or spin down drives to conform to the specification.

Step 2 – determining the region and zone configuration

Next, we need to decide on regions and zones. The number of regions stems from the desire to protect data from a disaster or to be closer to the sources that consume data. Once you have decided on the number of regions, pick the number of zones for each region. You need to have at least as many zones as replicas. We would recommend no less than three zones and Rackspace recommends five (`http://docs.openstack. org/havana/install-guide/install/apt/content/example-object-storage- installation-architecture.html`). Small clusters may be fine with four. Please refer to *Chapter 2, OpenStack Swift Architecture*, for a refresher on the definition of regions and zones.

Step 3 – choosing the account and container server configuration

As previously mentioned, unless you are installing a large configuration, you don't need to worry about a separate account and container servers. For a separate account and/or container servers, you need to ensure that the SQLite performance is adequate to meet your database listing and update needs by selecting the right amount of memory and flash. The OpenStack configuration guide recommends the following specifications (you may be able to reduce the requirements based on your cluster's size and performance requirements):

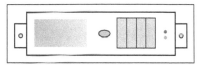

An optional account and a container server

- **Processor**: Dual quad-core.

- **Memory**: 8 to 12 GB.

- **Network I/O**: 1 x 1 Gbps NIC. Cost permitting, our recommendation would be to go beyond the official recommendation and use 10 Gbps.

- **Flash**: Not specified. This depends on user's performance requirements.

Step 4 – choosing the proxy server configuration

In general, the proxy server needs to keep up with the number of API requests. As discussed in *Chapter 2, OpenStack Swift Architecture*, additional middleware modules may also be running on the proxy server. Therefore, the proxy server needs a performance level that can keep up with this workload. Using a few powerful proxy servers as opposed to a large number of "wimpy" servers was proven to be more cost-effective by Zmanda (http://www.zmanda.com/blogs/?p=774). The OpenStack configuration guide seems to concur, and recommends the following specifications:

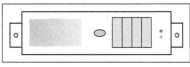

A proxy server

- **Processor**: Dual quad-core.
- **Network I/O**: A 1 x 1Gb/s NIC. Our recommendation would be to have at least two NICs, one for internal storage cluster connectivity and one for client (API) facing traffic. Cost permitting, our recommendation would be to go beyond the official recommendation and use 10 Gbps at least for internal storage cluster connectivity. Also see the related SSL discussion in the *Step 7 – choosing additional networking equipment* section that affects network I/O.

If your proxy server is running a lot of middleware modules, consider moving some of them to dedicated servers. The most common middleware to be separated is the auth software.

Step 5 – choosing the network hardware

There are three networks mentioned earlier — client (API) facing, internal storage cluster, and replication. See *Chapter 3, Installing OpenStack Swift* for an architecture view of the three networks. This might be a combination of 1 Gbps, 10 Gbps, or hybrid 1/10 Gbps ethernet switches. The following are some performance-related sizing techniques:

- **Client facing network**: The throughput requirement of the overall cluster dictates the network I/O for this network. For example, if your cluster has 10 proxy servers and is sized to satisfy 10,000 I/O requests per second of 1 MB size each, then clearly, each proxy server needs 10 Gbps network I/O capability.
- **Internal storage cluster**: The network requirements depend on the overall cluster throughput and size of the cluster. The size of the cluster matters since it will generate a large amount of postprocessing software component traffic (see *Chapter 2, OpenStack Swift Architecture*). As mentioned, cost permitting, we recommend the use of a 10 Gbps network.
- **Replication network**: This depends on the overall write throughput and the size of the cluster. For example, if you expect 1,000 write requests per second of 1 KB each, a 10 Mbps network might just work.

An additional consideration is the durability model. Since network switches take down entire zones or regions, unless you can service the failed switches rapidly, you might want to consider dual-redundant configurations. The following figure denotes a network switch:

A network switch

Step 6 – choosing the ratios of various server types

After selecting the individual server configurations, the ratios of different server types have to be chosen. Since most configurations will have only two types, that is, proxy and storage, we will only discuss the ratios of these two. According to work done by Zmanda, the proxy server should neither be underutilized nor overutilized. If the throughput of one storage server is 1 Gbps and that of the proxy server is 10 Gbps for example, then the ratio is 10 (this simple calculation applies to large objects dominated by throughput. For smaller objects, the calculation needs to focus on the number of requests).

Instead of buying hardware piecemeal, this ratio exercise allows a user to define a "unit" of purchase. The unit may be a full rack of hardware, multiple racks, or a few rack units. A unit of hardware is orthogonal to Swift zones, and typically you would want each unit to add capacity to every zone in a symmetric fashion. Each unit can have a set of proxy servers, storage servers, network switches, and so on defined in detail. Scaling the Swift cluster as data grows becomes a lot simpler using this technique of purchase. As mentioned earlier, you need to start with at least two proxies to provide for adequate durability.

For example, assume you want to grow your cluster in roughly 1 PB raw storage increments, with dense configurations. You might consider a unit of hardware with one proxy server, 2 x 10 Gbps switches, one management switch, and five storage servers with 60 drives of 4 TB each (that is, 240 TB x 5 = 1.2 PB). Given the previous comment regarding the need for at least two proxy servers, the initial installation would have to be 2.4 PB. With triple replication, the 1.2 PB raw storage translates to 400 TB usable storage. This example is not perfect because it may not fit cleanly within the rack boundaries, but it is meant to illustrate the point.

Step 7 – choosing additional networking equipment

The final step is to choose the load balancer, SSL acceleration hardware, and security appliances. A load balancer is required if there is more than one proxy node. Furthermore, you need to ensure that the load balancer is not a performance bottleneck. SSL hardware acceleration is required if most of the traffic is over secure HTTP (HTTPS) and the software SSL operation is overwhelming the proxy servers. Finally, security appliances such as IPS and IDS are required if the cloud is on the public Internet. Similar to the load balancer, these additional pieces of hardware must have enough performance to keep up with the aggregate proxy server's performance. The following figure denotes additional networking equipment needed for your Swift cluster:

Additional networking equipment

Step 8 – choosing a cloud gateway

This piece of equipment is the odd man out. It is not required to build an OpenStack Swift cluster. Instead, it is needed on premise (in case of a public cloud) or near the application (in case of a private cloud) if your application has not yet been ported to REST HTTP APIs. In this situation, the application is expecting a traditional block or file storage, which is the interface exposed by these cloud gateways. The gateway performs protocol translation and interfaces with the cloud on the other side. In addition to protocol translation, cloud gateways often add numerous other features such as WAN optimization, compression, deduplication, and encryption.

While most of this section has dealt with performance, there are other considerations as well, and these are covered in the next section.

Additional selection criteria

In addition to the previous criteria, the following items also need to be considered before finalizing hardware selection:

- **Durability**: Durability is a measure of reliability and is defined as 100 percent minus the probability of losing a 1 KB object in one year. Therefore, 99.999999999 percent durability (simply stated as 11 x 9 in this case) would imply that every year, you statistically lose one object if you have 100 billion 1 KB objects, or given 10,000 objects, expect a loss of a one object every 10,000,000 years. Calculating the durability of a Swift cluster is outside the scope of this book, but the selected hardware needs to meet your durability requirements. For users that require a high level of durability, low density enterprise-class disk drives, servers with dual fans and power supplies, and so on, are some considerations.

- **Availability**: Availability is defined as the percentage of time that requests are successfully processed by the cluster. Availability mostly impacts frontend network architecture in terms of having a single network (that is, a single point of failure) versus dual-redundant networks. As mentioned earlier, networks in a given zone can be single points of failure as long as your IT staff have the ability to troubleshoot them quickly.

- **Serviceability**: The serviceability of various pieces of hardware depends heavily on your strategy. If you choose fail-in-place (typically for large installations), serviceability is not a big concern. If you choose a repair/ servicing strategy (typically for small and medium installations), serviceability is a concern. Each device should lend itself to repair or servicing. A smaller scale installation may also force the choice of more expensive hardware In items of dual-redundant fans, power-supplies, and so on. The reason is that if there is a failure, there simply will not be too many back-off devices available for the Swift ring to choose from.

- **Manageability**: As previously discussed, servers come in all different types of flavors when it comes to hardware management and associated software. You should choose servers with management features that match your overall IT strategy.

The vendor selection strategy

If you really want to be like a web giant, you should buy hardware from ODMs and other commodity hardware manufacturers (either directly or through a systems integrator). However, in reality, the decision is not that simple. The questions you need to ask yourself are as follows:

Question	Yes for all questions	No for even one question
Can you specify the configuration of each server taking into account performance, durability, availability, serviceability, and manageability (versus needing vendor sales engineers to help)?		
Can you self-support (that is, if you get a 2 a.m. call, are you prepared to root-cause what happened versus calling the vendor)?	You are ready for commodity hardware!	You should stick with branded hardware.
Are you prepared to accept less sophisticated warranty, lead-times, end-of-life policies, and other terms?		
Can you live with minimal vendor-provided hardware management capabilities and software?		

Branded hardware

If you choose branded hardware, the process is fairly simple and involves issuing RFQs to your favorite server manufacturers such as HP, Dell, IBM, and FTS or to networking manufacturers such as Cisco, Juniper, and Arista, and choosing the one you like.

Commodity hardware

If you go down this route, there are numerous manufacturers to consider — Taiwanese ODMs and other storage hardware specialists such as Xyratex and Sanmina. Perhaps, the most interesting option to look at is an open source hardware movement called the **Open Compute Platform** (OCP).

According to their website, http://www.opencompute.org, OCP's mission is to design and enable the delivery of the most efficient server, storage, and datacenter hardware designs for scalable computing. All of OCP's work is in the open source. A number of manufacturers sell OCP-compliant hardware, and this compliance makes it somewhat simpler for users to choose consistent hardware across manufacturers.

The OCP Intel Motherboard Hardware v2.0, for example, supports two CPUs, four channels of DDR3 memory per CPU, a mini-SAS port for potential JBOD expansion, 1 Gbps network I/O, and a number of hardware-management features. It can also accept a PCIe mezzanine NIC card for a 10 Gbps network I/O. This server would be suitable for both the proxy and storage server (with different items populated).

The OCP OpenVault JBOD, as another example, is a 2U chassis that can hold up to 30 drives. This would make it a suitable companion for dense storage servers.

Summary

In this chapter, we have looked at the complex process of selecting hardware for an OpenStack Swift installation and the various trade-offs that can be made. In the next chapter, we will look at how to benchmark and tune our Swift cluster.

7
Tuning Your Swift Installation

OpenStack Swift's tremendous flexibility comes at a cost—it has a very large number of tuning options. Therefore, users utilizing Swift as a private cloud will need to tune their installation to optimize performance, durability, and availability for their unique workload. This chapter walks you through a performance benchmarking tool and the basics mechanisms available to tune your Swift cluster.

Performance benchmarking

There are several tools that can be used to benchmark the performance of your Swift cluster against a specific workload. **COSBench**, **ssbench**, and **swift-bench** are the most popular tools available. While swift-bench (`https://pypi.python.org/pypi/swift-bench/1.0`) used to be a part of the Swift project, and is therefore a common default benchmarking tool, this chapter discusses COSBench, given its completeness and the availability of graphical user interfaces with this tool.

COSBench is an open source distributed performance benchmarking tool for object storage systems. It is developed and maintained by Intel. COSBench supports a variety of object storage systems, including OpenStack Swift.

The physical configuration of COSBench is shown in the following diagram:

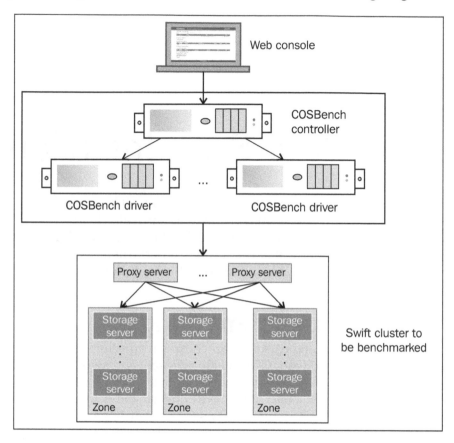

The key components of COSBench are:

- **Driver** (also referred to as COSBench driver or load generator):
  - Responsible for workload generation, issuing operations to target cloud object storage, and collecting performance statistics
  - In our test environment, the drivers were accessed via `http://10.27.128.14:18088/driver/index.html` and `http://10.27.128.15:18088/driver/index.html`

- **Controller** (also referred to as COSBench controller):

    ○ Responsible for coordinating drivers to collectively execute a workload, collecting and aggregating runtime status or benchmark results from driver instances, and accepting workload submissions

    ○ In our environment, the controller was accessed via `http://10.27.128.14:19088/controller/index.html`

A critical item to keep in mind as we start with COSBench is to ensure that the driver and controller machines do not inadvertently become performance bottlenecks. These nodes need to have adequate resources.

Next, the benchmark parameters are tied closely to your use case, and they need to be set accordingly. *Chapter 8, Additional Resources,* explores use cases in more detail, but a couple of benchmark-related examples are as follows:

- **Audio file sharing and collaboration**: This is a warm data use case, where you may want to set the ratio of read requests to write requests as relatively high, for example, 80 percent. The access rate for containers and objects may be relatively small (in tens of requests per second) with rather large objects (say a size of hundreds of MB or larger per object).

- **Document archiving**: This is a somewhat cold data use case, where you may want to set a relatively low read request to write request ratio, for example, 5 percent. The access rate for containers and objects may be high (in hundreds of requests per second) with medium size objects (say a size of 5 MB per object).

Keep these use cases in mind as we proceed.

In our test setup, COSBench was installed on a Ubuntu 12.04 operating system. The system also had JRE, unzip, and cURL installed *prior* to installing COSBench Version 0.3.3.0 (`https://github.com/intel-cloud/cosbench/releases/tag/0.3.3.0`). The installation is very simple as you will see in the following easy steps:

```
unzip 0.3.3.0.zip
ln -s 0.3.3.0/ cos
cd cos
chmod +x *.sh
```

More details on the installation and validation that the software has been installed correctly can be obtained from the COSBench user guide located at `https://github.com/intel-cloud/cosbench`. With the installation of COSBench, the user has access to a number of scripts. Some of these scripts are as follows:

- `start-all.sh` / `stop-all.sh`: Used to start/stop both controller and driver on the current node
- `start-controller.sh` / `stop-controller.sh`: Used to start/stop only controller on the current node
- `start-driver.sh` / `stop-driver.sh`: Used to start/stop only driver on the current node
- `cosbench-start.sh` / `cosbench-stop.sh`: These are internal scripts called by the preceding scripts
- `cli.sh`: Used to manipulate workload through command lines

The controller can be configured using the `conf/controller.conf` file, and the driver can be configured using the `conf/driver.conf` file.

The drivers can be started on all the driver nodes using the `start-driver.sh` script, while the controller can be started on the controller node using the `start-controller.sh` script.

Next, we need to create **workloads**. A workload can be considered as one complete benchmark test. A `workload` consists of **workstages**. Each `workstage` consists of **work** items. Finally, `work` items consist of **operations**. A `workload` can have more than one `workstage` that is executed sequentially. A `workstage` can have more than one `work` item that are executed in parallel.

There is one normal type (`main`) and four special types (`init`, `prepare`, `cleanup`, and `dispose`) of `work`. Type `main` is where we will spend the rest of this discussion; the key parameters for this phase are as follows:

- `workers` is used to specify the number of workers used to conduct work in parallel, and thus control the load generated
- `runtime` (plus `rampup` and `rampdown`), `totalOps`, and `totalBytes` are used to control other parameters of the load generated, including how to start and end the `work`

The `main` phase has the operations of `read`, `write`, and `delete`. You will typically want to specify the number of containers and objects to be written, and the object sizes. Numbers and sizes are specified as expressions, and a variety of options, such as constant, uniform, and sequential, are available.

The workload is specified as an XML file. We will now create a workload that is fashioned after the document archiving use case discussed earlier. It uses a workload ratio of 95 percent writes and 5 percent reads. The drivers will spawn 128 workers for the duration of one hour; the object size is static at 5 MB and 100 objects will be created. The workload is as follows:

```xml
<?xml version="1.0" encoding="UTF-8"?>
<workload name="LTS2-UAT-V1-128W-5MB-Baseline" description="LTS2 UAT
workload configuration">
<auth type="swauth" config=" ;password=xxxx;url= >username=8016-
2588:evault-user@evault.com https://auth.lts2.evault.com/v1.0"/
<storage type="swift" config=""/>
  <workflow>
    <workstage name="init" closuredelay="0">
      <work name="init" type="init" workers="16" interval="20"
      division="container" runtime="0" rampup="0" rampdown="0"
      totalOps="1" totalBytes="0" config="containers=r(1,32)">
        <operation type="init" ratio="100" division-"container"
        config="objects=r(0,0);sizes=c(0)B;containers=r(1,32)"
          id="none"/>
      </work>
    </workstage>
    <workstage name="prepare" closuredelay="0">
      <work name="prepare" type="prepare" workers="16"
        interval="20"
      division="object" runtime="0" rampup="0" rampdown="0"
      totalOps="1" totalBytes="0"
        config="containers=r(1,32);objects=r(1,50);
        sizes=u(5,5)MB">
        <operation type="prepare" ratio="100" division="object"
        config="createContainer=false;containers=r(1,32);
          objects=r(1,50);sizes-u(5,5)MB" id="none"/>
      </work>
    </workstage>
    <workstage name="normal" closuredelay="0">
      <work name="normal" type="normal" workers="128"
        interval="20"
      division="none" runtime="300" rampup="100" rampdown="0"
      totalOps="0" totalBytes="0">
        <operation type="read" ratio="5" division="none"
        config="containers=u(1,32);objects=u(1,50);" id="none"/>
        <operation type="write" ratio="95" division="none"
        config="containers=u(1,32);objects=u(51,100);
          sizes=u(5,5)MB"
        id="none"/>
```

```
        </work>
      </workstage>
      <workstage name="cleanup" closuredelay="0">
        <work name="cleanup" type="cleanup" workers="16"
          interval="20"
        division="object" runtime="0" rampup="0" rampdown="0"
        totalOps="1" totalBytes="0"
          config="containers=r(1,32);objects=r(1,100);">
<         operation type="cleanup" ratio="100" division="object"
        config="deleteContainer=false;containers=r(1,32);
          objects=r(1,100);" id="none"/>
        </work>
      </workstage>
      <workstage name="dispose" closuredelay="0">
        <work name="dispose" type="dispose" workers="16"
          interval="20"
        division="container" runtime="0" rampup="0" rampdown="0"
        totalOps="1" totalBytes="0" config="containers=r(1,32);">
          <operation type="dispose" ratio="100"
          division="container"
          config="objects=r(0,0);sizes=c(0)B;containers=r(1,32);"
            id="none"/>
        </work>
      </workstage>
    </workflow>
  </workload>
```

The result of `workload` is a series of reported metrics: throughput as measured by operations/second, response time measured by average duration between operation start to end, bandwidth as measured by MBps, success ratio (percentage successful), and other metrics. A sample unrelated report is shown in the following screenshot:

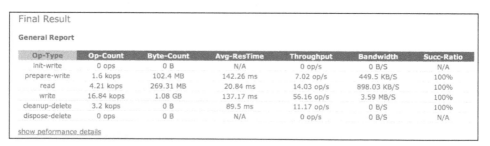

If the Swift cluster under test stands up to your `workload`, you are done. You may want to perform some basic tuning, but this is optional. However, if the Swift cluster is unable to cope with your `workload`, you need to perform tuning.

The first step is to identify bottlenecks. See *Chapter 5*, *Managing Swift*, for tools to find performance bottlenecks. Nagios or swift-recon may be particularly well suited for this. Of course, simple tools such as top may be used as well. Once you isolate the bottleneck to particular server(s) and the underlying components such as CPU performance, memory, I/O, disk bandwidth, and response times, we can move to the next step, which is tuning.

Hardware tuning

Chapter 6, *Choosing the Right Hardware*, discusses the hardware considerations in great detail. It is sufficient to say that choosing the right hardware can have a huge impact on your performance, durability, availability, and cost.

Software tuning

In *Chapter 2*, *OpenStack Swift Architecture*, we talked about Swift using two types of software modules — data path (referred to as **WSGI servers** in Swift documentation) and postprocessing (referred to as **background daemons**). In addition, there is the ring. All three merit different considerations in terms of software tuning. Also, we will briefly look at some additional tuning considerations.

The ring considerations

The number of **partitions** in a ring affects performance and needs to be chosen carefully because this cannot be changed easily. Swift documentation recommends a minimum of 100 partitions per drive to ensure even distribution across servers. Taking the maximum anticipated number of drives multiplied by 100 and then rounded up to the nearest power of two provides the minimum number of total partitions. Using a number higher than is needed will mean extremely uniform distribution, but at the cost of performance, since more partitions put a higher burden on replicators and other postprocessing jobs. Therefore, users should not overestimate the ultimate size of the cluster.

For example, let us assume that we expect our cluster to have a maximum of 1,000 nodes each with 60 disks. That gives us *60 x 1,000 x 100 = 6,000,000* partitions. Rounded up to the nearest power of two, we get *2^23 = 8,388,608*. The value that will be used to create the ring will therefore be 23. We did not discuss the disk size in this computation, but a cluster with smaller/faster disks (for example, a 2 TB SAS drive) will perform better than clusters with larger/slower disks (for example, a 6 TB SATA drive) with the same number of partitions.

Data path software tuning

The key data path software modules are proxy, account, container, and object servers. There are literally dozens of tuning parameters, but the four most important ones in terms of performance impact are as follows:

Parameter	Proxy server	Storage server
`workers` (auto by default)	Each worker can handle a `max_clients` number of simultaneous requests. Ideally, having more `workers` means more requests can be handled without being blocked. However, there is an upper limit dictated by the CPU. Start by setting `workers` as 2 multiplied by the number of cores. If the storage server includes account, container, and object servers, you may have to do some experimentation.	
`max_clients` (1024 by default)	Since we want the most effective use of network capacity, we want a large number of simultaneous requests. You probably won't need to change the default setting.	In data published by RedHat, filesystem calls were found to block an entire worker. This means that having a very large setting for `max_clients` is not useful. Experiment with this parameter, and don't be afraid to reduce this number all the way down to match `threads_per_disk` or even 1.
`object_chunk_size` (64 KB by default)	Given that this data is flowing over an internal Swift network, a larger setting may be more efficient. RedHat found 2 MB to be more efficient than the default size when using a 10 Gbps network.	N/A
`threads_per_disk` (0 by default)	N/A	This parameter defines the size of the per-disk thread pool. A default value of 0 means a per-disk thread pool will not be used. In general, Swift documentation recommends keeping this small to prevent large queue depths that result in high read latencies. Try starting with four threads per disk.

Postprocessing software tuning

The impact of tuning postprocessing software is very different from data path software. The focus is not so much on servicing API requests, but rather on reliability, performance, and consistency. Increasing the rate of operations for replicators and auditors makes the system more durable, since this reduces the time required to find and fix faults, at the expense of increased server load. Also, increasing the auditor rate reduces consistency windows by putting a higher server load. The following are the parameters to consider:

- concurrency: Swift documentation (http://docs.openstack.org/developer/swift/deployment_guide.html) recommends setting the concurrency of most postprocessing jobs at 1, except for replicators where they recommend 2. If you need a higher level of durability, consider increasing this number. Durability, again, is measured by 1–P (object loss in a year), where the object size is typically 1 KB.

- interval: Unless you want to reduce the load on servers, increase reliability, or reduce consistency windows, you probably want to stick with the default value.

Additional tuning parameters

A number of additional tuning parameters are available to the user. The important ones are listed as follows:

- **memcached**: A number of Swift services rely on memcached to cache lookups since Swift does not cache any object data. While memcached can be run on any server, it should be turned on for all proxy servers. If memcached is turned on, please ensure adequate RAM and CPU resources are available.

- **System time**: Given that Swift is a distributed system, the timestamp of an object is used for a number of reasons. Therefore, it is important to ensure that time is consistent between servers. Services such as NTP may be used for this purpose.

- **Filesystem**: Swift is filesystem agnostic; however, XFS is the one tested by the Swift community. It is important to keep a high inode size, for example, 1024 to ensure that default and some additional metadata can be stored efficiently. Other parameters should be set as described in *Chapter 3, Installing OpenStack Swift*.

- **Operating system**: General operating system tuning is outside the scope of this book. However, Swift documentation suggests disabling TIME_WAIT and syn cookies and doubling the amount of allowed conntrack in sysctl. conf. Since the OS is usually installed on a disk that is not part of storage drives, you may want to consider a small SSD to get fast boot times.

- **Network stack**: Network stack tuning is also outside the scope of this book. However, there may be some additional obvious tuning, for example, enabling jumbo frames for the internal storage cluster network. Jumbo frames may also be enabled on the client facing or replication network if this traffic is over the LAN (in the case of private clouds).

- **Logging**: Unless custom log handlers are used, Swift logs directly to syslog. Swift generates a large amount of log data, and therefore, managing logs correctly is extremely important. Setting logs appropriately can impact both performance and your ability to diagnose problems. You may want to consider high performance variants such as rsyslog (http://www.rsyslog. com/) or syslog-ng (http://www.balabit.com/network-security/syslog-ng/opensource-logging-system).

Summary

In this chapter, we reviewed how to benchmark a Swift cluster and tune it for a specific use case for private cloud users. The next and final chapter covers use cases appropriate for OpenStack Swift and additional resources.

8
Additional Resources

Having acquired the knowhow on building, managing, and tuning OpenStack clusters by reading the preceding chapters, you are now ready to join the global elite group of OpenStack Swift experts and take your career to the next step. Let's now explore a few use cases of OpenStack Swift and get pointers to useful resources.

Use cases

Use cases for OpenStack Swift may be put into three broad categories, namely, **service providers** (public cloud storage), **Web 2.0** (private cloud storage for enterprises, wherein features and functionality are delivered via a web interface), and **enterprises** (private/public cloud storage).

- Public Cloud Storage
- IaaS offering

Service Providers

- Private Cloud Storage
- Storage to run their site

Web 2.0s

- Private Cloud Storage
- Long-term storage in a public cloud

Enterprises

3 Use-Cases for OpenStack Swift

Service providers

Amazon's S3 broke ground as the pioneer in cloud storage. A large number of service providers have entered or are looking to enter this new product category, and OpenStack Swift offers them a viable option that will meet their customers' **service level agreement (SLA)** needs. OpenStack Swift is a mature production-ready open source technology available for creating public cloud storage. It is cost effective, extensible, and meets availability and performance metrics for such a service.

Service providers can target small- to large-sized businesses since a public cloud can prove economical and hassle-free for them. They can also target consumers who want to archive their data or save it in a public space for collaboration needs. Service providers can tap into the benefits of cloud storage ranging from elimination of capital expenditures for users to elimination of hardware and software management and elimination of capacity planning. Service providers creating public cloud storage may want to focus on particular applications, for example, backup, medical record keeping, expense reports, or verticals (such as county/city governments, libraries, hospitals, or specific geographies).

Web 2.0

Web 2.0 sites such as Twitter, Pinterest, Tumblr, and Wikipedia used a public cloud for computing and storage in their early stages. However, as they grew, they hit a point where it was more economical and secure to have their own private cloud. Some of them also required an infrastructure that ensured better performance and gave them more control over what a public cloud could offer. At that point, moving to a private cloud using OpenStack Swift with S3 APIs provided a smooth transition.

Enterprises

Enterprises are generally heavily invested in their existing storage infrastructure that has especially been built to adhere to strict standards of reliability, availability, and serviceability, while providing fast access times. All their software is geared to SAN- or NAS-based architecture and the new RESTful storage APIs are alien to them. So, on the face of it, an enterprise may not see much value in moving to a private cloud. On the contrary, enterprises may derive tremendous value out of both public and private cloud storage. With the latest Big Data trend of saving everything, enterprises' need for cheap data storage is growing exponentially. A public cloud tuned for long-term storage may save cost, provide convenient access, and protect data better than anything the enterprise is using currently. In a similar vein, a compelling argument for moving to a private cloud is the fact that its architecture is very compatible with Big Data applications, including the use of MapReduce algorithms.

In the use cases pointed to in the following tables, we will see examples of companies that store data such as medical images, bioinformatics data, banking records, oil and gas data, logs, and internal corporate videos. Finally, an enterprise may consider both a private and a public cloud to store the primary copy on premise and secondary copy in different locations. The additional copy in the public cloud serves as a backup, and it will be available for recovery as needed.

Transitioning to the cloud, as discussed in *Chapter 1, Cloud Storage: Why Can't I be like Google?*, it is not as formidable as it may seem at first. Several applications support Swift or S3 APIs natively, easing the transition to OpenStack Swift. Cloud gateways are another popular mechanism to ease this transition. Finally, an enterprise may consider developing new applications in Python, PHP, and Ruby-on-Rails-based paradigms that can directly interface to a private or public cloud.

Operating systems used for OpenStack implementations

OpenStack supports a variety of operating systems and we have compiled a table listing the operating systems used in some of the OpenStack implementations. The following table provides information on organizations using these operating systems in their implementations:

Operating system	Implementation / organization	Link
Ubuntu	NeCTAR, MercadoLibre, Intel, Opscode, Liveperson	`https://www.openstack.org/user-stories/nectar/`
		`https://www.openstack.org/user-stories/mercadolibre/`
		`https://www.openstack.org/summit/openstack-summit-hong-kong-2013/session-videos/presentation/openstack-deployment-with-chef-workshop`
		`https://www.openstack.org/summit/openstack-summit-hong-kong-2013/session-videos/presentation/is-open-source-good-enough-a-deep-study-of-swift-and-ceph-performance`
		`https://www.openstack.org/summit/openstack-summit-hong-kong-2013/session-videos/presentation/liveperson-openstack-case-study-from-0-to-100-in-1-year`

Operating system	Implementation / organization	Link
Redhat	CERN	https://www.openstack.org/user-stories/cern/
CentOS	Workday	https://www.openstack.org/summit/openstack-summit-hong-kong-2013/session-videos/presentation/workday-on-openstack
HP Cloud OS	HP	https://www.openstack.org/summit/openstack-summit-hong-kong-2013/session-videos/presentation/is-open-source-good-enough-a-deep-study-of-swift-and-ceph-performance
Debian	eNovance	http://www.openstack.org/user-stories/enovance/

Virtualization used for OpenStack implementations

OpenStack services can be installed on virtual machines created using ESX, KVM, Hyper-V, and so on. The following table lists the virtualization technology used in a few implementations:

Virtualization	Implementation / organization	Link
KVM	eNovance, Workday, CERN	https://www.openstack.org/summit/openstack-summit-hong-kong-2013/session-videos/presentation/ceph-the-de-facto-storage-backend-for-openstack
		https://www.openstack.org/summit/openstack-summit-hong-kong-2013/session-videos/presentation/workday-on-openstack
		https://www.openstack.org/user-stories/cern/
VMWare	VMWare	https://www.openstack.org/summit/openstack-summit-hong-kong-2013/session-videos/presentation/hands-on-with-openstack-vsphere

Provisioning and distribution tools

The most common provisioning and deployment tools used to deploy OpenStack are Puppet, Chef, and Juju. The following table lists the tools and some of the OpenStack installations that they are used in:

Provisioning/ Deployment	Implementation / Organization	Link
Puppet	CERN, NeCTAR, Kickstart, Cisco Webex, Liveperson	https://www.openstack.org/user-stories/cern/
		https://www.openstack.org/user-stories/nectar/
		https://www.openstack.org/summit/openstack-summit-hong-kong-2013/session-videos/presentation/kickstack-rapid-openstack-deployment-with-puppet
		https://www.openstack.org/user-stories/cisco-webex/
		http://www.openstack.org/user-stories/liveperson/
Chef	Workday, Opscode, MercadoLibre	https://www.openstack.org/summit/openstack-summit-hong-kong-2013/session-videos/presentation/workday-on-openstack
		https://www.openstack.org/summit/openstack-summit-hong-kong-2013/session-videos/presentation/openstack-deployment-with-chef-workshop
		https://www.openstack.org/user-stories/mercadolibre/
Juju	VMWare	https://www.openstack.org/summit/openstack-summit-hong-kong-2013/session-videos/presentation/vmware-and-openstack-bridging-the-divide-using-ubuntu-and-juju
Compass	Huawei	https://www.openstack.org/summit/openstack-summit-hong-kong-2013/session-videos/presentation/compass-yet-another-openstack-deployment-system

Monitoring and graphing tools

The following table lists tools that can be used, in addition to OpenStack Swift, to enable monitoring (some of them are mentioned in prior chapters too):

Monitoring tool	Download tool	Organization implementations
Groundwork	`http://sourceforge.net/projects/gwmos/`	NeCTAR: `http://www.openstack.org/user-stories/nectar/`
Ganglia: Graphing tool	`http://sourceforge.net/apps/trac/ganglia/wiki/ganglia_quick_start`	CERN: `https://www.youtube.com/watch?v=jRkTVh27XBQ`
Graphite	`https://github.com/etsy/statsd/blob/master/docs/graphite.md`	Rackspace: `https://www.openstack.org/summit/openstack-summit-hong-kong-2013/session-videos/presentation/an-intimate-look-at-running-openstack-swift-at-scale`
Zabbix	`http://www.patlathem.com/zabbix-beginners-guide-installing-and-configuring-the-monitoring-server/`	
NagiOS	`http://www.nagios.org/download`	Redhat, Mirantis, Dell crowbar

Additional information

The following links provide additional information on OpenStack Swift:

- `http://swift.openstack.org`
- `https://github.com/openstack/swift`

The following blogs provide more up-to-date information on the topics discussed in this chapter; they also provide more updated user stories, OpenStack implementations by customers, deployment tools, monitoring and graphing tools, and more information related to OpenStack implementations:

- `http://www.buildcloudstorage.com/2014/03/swift-book.html`
- `http://www.vedams.com/blog/cloud/`

Additional support, including mailing lists, is available at the following links, and users have the ability to review previously answered questions or post new questions to the community via launchpad:

- `http://www.openstack.org/community/`
- `http://www.openstack.org/blog/`
- `https://swiftstack.com/blog/`
- `https://launchpad.net/swift`
- `https://www.mail-archive.com/openstack@lists.openstack.org/`

Summary

As we can see from our discussion in this chapter, OpenStack Swift is relevant to every user segment, from the individual consumer to the large service provider. Service providers offer value added public clouds, Web2.0s build private clouds to house all their user data, and enterprises use public clouds and create private secure clouds to archive their data and run analytics.

At this point, we hope you have a good idea of what cloud storage is and how OpenStack can be used to create cloud storage. We hope you are confident in terms of how to install, manage, and use OpenStack Swift, including some finer points such as hardware selection and performance tuning. It is now time to get involved with the OpenStack Swift community as a user, contributor, or evangelist.

Advanced Features

This appendix provides details on the set of commands that can be run from a Swift CLI session. These commands can be used to perform CRUD operations.

Commands

The commands that can be run from the Swift CLI are `list`, `stat`, `post`, `upload`, `download`, and `delete`. Each command has detailed help, which can be displayed by running the `swift command -h` command, for example, `swift list -h`.

List

The `list` command is used to list the containers for the account or the objects for a container. This subsection describes the usage of the `list` command.

```
# swift list <container> -A Auth_URL -U User -K Key --os-username=<auth-
user-name> --os-password=<auth-password> --os-tenant-id=<auth-tenant-
id> --os-tenant-name=<auth-tenant-name> --os-auth-url=<auth-url> --os-
auth-token=<auth-token> --os-storage-url=<storage-url> --os-region-
name=<region-name> --os-service-type=<service-type>  --os-endpoint-
type=<endpoint-type> --prefix=PREFIX
```

Examples

You can list the containers with size information, using the following commands:

```
# swift -V 2.0 -A https://auth.lts2.evault.com/v2.0 -U admin:user1 -K t1
list --lh
# swift -V 2.0 -A https://auth.lts2.evault.com/v2.0 -U admin:user1 -K t1
list -long
```

You can list the containers with size information and a prefix of con1 by using the following command:

```
# swift -V 2.0 -A https://auth.lts2.evault.com/v2.0 -U admin:user1 -K t1
list --lh --prefix con1
```

You can list the containers with size information and a prefix of con1 in the region regionOne by using the following command:

```
# swift -V 2.0 -A https://auth.lts2.evault.com/v2.0 -U admin:user1 -K t1
list --lh --prefix con1 --os-region-name=regionOne
```

Stat

The stat command is used to display information for an account, container, or object. This section describes the usage of the stat command.

```
# swift stat <container> <object> -A Auth_URL -U User -K Key --os-
username=<auth-user-name> --os-password=<auth-password> --os-tenant-
id=<auth-tenant-id> --os-tenant-name=<auth-tenant-name> --os-auth-
url=<auth-url> --os-auth-token=<auth-token> --os-storage-url=<storage-
url> --os-region-name=<region-name> --os-service-type=<service-type>
--os-endpoint-type=<endpoint-type>
```

Examples

Display the metadata of the account by using the following command:

```
# swift -V 2.0 -A https://auth.lts2.evault.com/v2.0 -U admin: user1 -K t1
stat
```

Display the metadata of the container2 container by using the following command:

```
# swift -V 2.0 -A https://auth.lts2.evault.com/v2.0 -U admin:user1 -K t1
stat container2
```

Display the metadata of the key.txt object in the container3 container by using the following command:

```
# swift -V 2.0 -A https://auth.lts2.evault.com/v2.0 -U admin:user1 -K t1
stat container3 key.txt
```

Display the metadata of the account in the regionOne region in long format with totals by using the following command:

```
# swift -V 2.0 -A https://auth.lts2.evault.com/v2.0 -U admin:user1 -K t1
stat --lh  --os-region-name=regionOne
```

Post

The post command is used to update metadata information for the account, container, or object. This section describes the usage of the post command.

```
# swift post <container> <object> --read-acl <acl> --write-acl <acl>
--meta <name:value> --header <header> -A Auth_URL -U User -K Key --os-
username=<auth-user-name> --os-password=<auth-password> --os-tenant-
id=<auth-tenant-id> --os-tenant-name=<auth-tenant-name> --os-auth-
url=<auth-url> --os-auth-token=<auth-token> --os-storage-url=<storage-
url> --os-region-name=<region-name> --os-service-type=<service-type>
--os-endpoint-type=<endpoint-type>
```

Examples

Update the read-acl metadata for the container1 container by using the following command:

```
# swift -V 2.0 -A https://auth.lts2.evault.com/v2.0 -U admin:user1 -K t1
post container1 --read-acl=account1
```

Add metadata Size:Large and Color:Blue to the container2 container by using the following command:

```
# swift -V 2.0 -A https://auth.lts2.evault.com/v2.0 -U admin:user1 -K t1
post container2 -m Size:Large -m Color:Blue
```

Update the content-type header metadata as text/plain for the container3 container by using the following command:

```
# swift -V 2.0 -A https://auth.lts2.evault.com/v2.0 -U admin:user1 -K t1
post container3 -H "content-type:text/plain"
```

Update the read-acl metadata for the container4 container by accessing through the regionOne region:

```
# swift -V 2.0 -A https://auth.lts2.evault.com/v2.0 -U admin:user1 -K t1
post container4 --read-acl=account1 --os-region-name=regionOne
```

Upload

The upload command is used to upload specified files and directories to the given container. This section describes the usage of the upload command.

```
# swift upload <container> <file_or_directory> --changed --segment-
size <size> --segment-container <container> --leave-segments --header
<header> -A Auth_URL -U User -K Key --os-username=<auth-user-name> --os-
password=<auth-password> --os-tenant-id=<auth-tenant-id> --os-tenant-
name=<auth-tenant-name> --os-auth-url=<auth-url> --os-auth-token=<auth-
token> --os-storage-url=<storage-url> --os-region-name=<region-name>
--os-service-type=<service-type>   --os-endpoint-type=<endpoint-type>
```

Examples

Upload the key.txt object to the container1 container by using the following command:

```
# swift -V 2.0 -A https://auth.lts2.evault.com/v2.0 -U admin:user1 -K t1
upload container1 key.txt
```

Upload multiple objects (key1.txt, key2.txt, and key3.txt) to the container1 container by using the following command:

```
# swift -V 2.0 -A https://auth.lts2.evault.com/v2.0 -U admin:user1 -K t1
upload container1 key1.txt key2.txt key3.txt
```

Upload the key.txt object to the container2 container using a segment size (segment-size) of 100 bytes. Swift has an object size limit of 5 GB by default. Larger files can be uploaded by using the segment-size option. The object will be stored as multiple segments in the Swift object store. In this example, each segment created will be of 100 bytes, and there will be several such segments uploaded, based on size of the object. The -changed option is used to upload the file only if this file has changed from when it was last uploaded, as in the following command:

```
# swift -V 2.0 -A https://auth.lts2.evault.com/v2.0 -U admin:user1 -K t1
upload container2 key.txt --changed --segment-size=100
```

Upload the key.txt object to the container3 container using a segment size (segment-size) of 100 bytes. Also, we explicitly specify the seg_container3 segment folder to where the segments will be uploaded.

```
# swift -V 2.0 -A https://auth.lts2.evault.com/v2.0 -U admin:user1 -K t1
upload container3 key.txt --segment-size=100 --segment-container=seg_
container3
```

Upload the `key.txt` object to the `container4` container using a segment size (`segment-size`) of 100 bytes. The `use-slo` option is specified to create a static large object instead of the default dynamic large object, as shown in the following command:

```
# swift -V 2.0 -A https://auth.lts2.evault.com/v2.0 -U admin:user1 -K
t1 upload container4 key.txt --segment-size=100 --use-slo --os-region-
name=regionOne
```

Download

The `download` command is used to download objects from containers. This section describes the usage of the `download` command.

```
# swift download <container> <object> --all --prefix <prefix> --output
<out_file> -A Auth_URL -U User -K Key --os-username=<auth-user-
name> --os-password=<auth-password> --os-tenant-id=<auth-tenant-id>
--os-tenant-name=<auth-tenant-name> --os-auth-url=<auth-url> --os-
auth-token=<auth-token> --os-storage-url=<storage-url> --os-region-
name=<region-name> --os-service-type=<service-type>  --os-endpoint-
type=<endpoint-type>
```

Examples

Download all objects from all the containers by using the following command:

```
# swift -V 2.0 -A https://auth.lts2.evault.com/v2.0 -U admin:user1 -K t1
download --all
```

Download all objects with the `key` prefix from the `container1` container by using the following command:

```
# swift -V 2.0 -A https://auth.lts2.evault.com/v2.0 -U admin:user1 -K t1
download container1 --prefix key
```

Download the `key.txt` object from the `container1` container by using the following command:

```
# swift -V 2.0 -A https://auth.lts2.evault.com/v2.0 -U admin:user1 -K t1
download container1 key.txt
```

Download all objects from all the containers utilizing two threads for object download by using the following command:

```
# swift -V 2.0 -A https://auth.lts2.evault.com/v2.0 -U admin:user1 -K t1
download --all --object-threads 2 --os-region-name=regionOne
```

Delete

The `delete` command is used to delete a container or delete objects within a container. This section describes the usage of the `delete` command.

```
# swift delete <container> <object> --all –leave_segments -A Auth_URL
-U User –K Key --os-username=<auth-user-name> --os-password=<auth-
password> --os-tenant-id=<auth-tenant-id> --os-tenant-name=<auth-tenant-
name> --os-auth-url=<auth-url> --os-auth-token=<auth-token> --os-
storage-url=<storage-url> --os-region-name=<region-name> --os-service-
type=<service-type>  --os-endpoint-type=<endpoint-type>
```

Examples

Delete the `key.txt` object from the `container1` container by using the following command:

```
# swift -V 2.0 -A https://auth.lts2.evault.com/v2.0 -U admin:user1 -K t1
delete container1 key.txt
```

Delete all objects from the container2 container, and leave the segments as is, by using the following command:

```
# swift -V 2.0 -A https://auth.lts2.evault.com/v2.0 -U admin:user1 -K t1
delete container2 --leave-segments
```

Delete all the objects and all the containers by using the following command:

```
# swift -V 2.0 -A https://auth.lts2.evault.com/v2.0 -U admin:user1 -K t1
delete --all
```

Delete all the objects and all the containers utilizing two threads for deleting objects by using the following command:

```
# swift -V 2.0 -A https://auth.lts2.evault.com/v2.0 -U admin:user1 -K t1
delete --all --object-threads=2  --os-region-name=regionOne
```

Index

K

Keystone
  installing 39-43
Keystone auth 23
Keystone service
  Keystone, installing 39-43
  MySQL, installing 38, 39
  using 38

L

LAN-on-motherboard (LOM) 76
large objects
  transferring 55
list command
  about 105
  examples 105, 106
logging
  about 24
  rsyslog, used 67
logical organization, objects 15, 16

M

manageability 83
metadata
  displaying, cURL used 47
  displaying, REST API used 48
  displaying, Swift Client CLI used 47
  updating, REST API used 51
  updating, Swift Client CLI used 51
migrations 72
monitoring tools
  using 102
MySQL
  installing 38, 39

N

Nagios
  about 62
  URL 62
network
  public network, configuring 28
  storage network, configuring 28
network hardware
  client facing network 80

internal storage cluster 80
  replication network 80
  selecting 80, 81
network interface card (NIC) 76
network replication
  configuring 29
new drives
  adding 71
new storage
  adding 71
node failure
  handling 69
  proxy server failure 70

O

object expirer 22
objects
  listing, cURL used 50
  listing, REST API used 50
  logical organization 15, 16
object server 19
object storage
  about 10, 11
  automating management tasks 11
  benefits 11
  data placement 11
OCP Intel Motherboard Hardware v2.0 85
OCP OpenVault JBOD 85
Open Compute Platform (OCP)
  about 84
  URL 84
OpenStack configuration guide
  URL 78
OpenStack Swift
  about 12, 13
  accessing, Amazon S3 API commands
    used 58
  accessing, jclouds library used 59
  accessing, python-swiftclient library
    used 60
  accessing, ruby-openstack library used 60
  additional features 25
  deploying, provisioning/distribution tools
    used 101
  downloading 30
  functionality 12

Thank you for buying
Implementing Cloud Storage with OpenStack Swift

About Packt Publishing

Packt, pronounced 'packed', published its first book "*Mastering phpMyAdmin for Effective MySQL Management*" in April 2004 and subsequently continued to specialize in publishing highly focused books on specific technologies and solutions.

Our books and publications share the experiences of your fellow IT professionals in adapting and customizing today's systems, applications, and frameworks. Our solution based books give you the knowledge and power to customize the software and technologies you're using to get the job done. Packt books are more specific and less general than the IT books you have seen in the past. Our unique business model allows us to bring you more focused information, giving you more of what you need to know, and less of what you don't.

Packt is a modern, yet unique publishing company, which focuses on producing quality, cutting-edge books for communities of developers, administrators, and newbies alike. For more information, please visit our website: www.packtpub.com.

About Packt Open Source

In 2010, Packt launched two new brands, Packt Open Source and Packt Enterprise, in order to continue its focus on specialization. This book is part of the Packt Open Source brand, home to books published on software built around Open Source licences, and offering information to anybody from advanced developers to budding web designers. The Open Source brand also runs Packt's Open Source Royalty Scheme, by which Packt gives a royalty to each Open Source project about whose software a book is sold.

Writing for Packt

We welcome all inquiries from people who are interested in authoring. Book proposals should be sent to author@packtpub.com. If your book idea is still at an early stage and you would like to discuss it first before writing a formal book proposal, contact us; one of our commissioning editors will get in touch with you.

We're not just looking for published authors; if you have strong technical skills but no writing experience, our experienced editors can help you develop a writing career, or simply get some additional reward for your expertise.

OpenStack Cloud Computing Cookbook

Second Edition

ISBN: 978-1-78216-758-7   Paperback: 396 pages

Over 100 recipes to successfully set up and manage your OpenStack cloud environments with complete coverage of Nova, Swift, Keystone, Glance, Horizon, Neutron, and Cinder

1. Updated for OpenStack Grizzly.

2. Learn how to install, configure, and manage all of the OpenStack core projects including new topics such as block storage and software defined networking.

Python 3
Object Oriented Programming

ISBN: 978-1-84951-126-1   Paperback: 404 pages

Harness the power of Python 3 objects

1. Learn how to do Object Oriented Programming in Python using this step-by-step tutorial.

2. Design public interfaces using abstraction, encapsulation, and information hiding.

3. Turn your designs into working software by studying the Python syntax.

4. Raise, handle, define, and manipulate exceptions using special error objects.

Please check **www.PacktPub.com** for information on our titles

RESTful PHP
Web Services

Learn the basic architectural concepts and steps through examples of consuming and creating RESTful web services in PHP

Samisa Abeysinghe

PACKT

RESTful PHP
Web Services

ISBN: 978-1-84719-552-4   Paperback: 220 pages

Learn the basic architectural concepts and steps through examples of consuming and creating RESTful web services in PHP

1. Get familiar with REST principles.

2. Learn how to design and implement PHP web services with REST.

3. Real-world examples, with services and client PHP code snippets.

4. Introduces tools and frameworks that can be used when developing RESTful PHP applications.

Apache CloudStack
Cloud Computing

Leverage the power of CloudStack and learn to extend the CloudStack environment

Nevin Sabharwal
Ravi Shankar

PACKT

Apache CloudStack Cloud Computing

ISBN: 978-1-78216-010-6   Paperback: 294 pages

Leverage the power of CloudStack and learn to extend the CloudStack environment

1. Install, deploy, and manage a cloud service using CloudStack.

2. Step-by-step instructions on setting up and running the leading open source cloud platform, CloudStack.

3. Set up an IaaS cloud environment using CloudStack.

Please check **www.PacktPub.com** for information on our titles

9 781782 168058